HAPPY TO BE HERE

HAPPY TO BE HERE
A Transplant Takes Root in Farmville, Virginia

Collected columns from The Farmville Herald

by Karen A. Bellenir

Pier Press, Farmville, VA

This book contains columns that were printed in *The Farmville Herald* over a seven-year period, from August 2009 through July 2016. Most of them are reprinted as they originally appeared. In a few instances, especially related to events that have passed, information has been updated.

© 2016 Karen A. Bellenir. All rights reserved.
Other than brief quotations used for review purposes,
no part of this book may be used or reproduced in any manner
without prior written permission. For permissions assistance,
please contact the publisher at info@pierpress.com.

Pier Press, LLC
P.O. Box 366
Farmville, VA 23901
PierPress.com

ISBN 978-0-9916551-9-9 (pbk)
ISBN 978-0-9969915-0-6 (ebook)

Cover and interior design by Buffy Bellenir • www.buffybellenir.com

CONTENTS

Prelude 3
    Why Farmville *(August 2009)*

Happy New Year! 5
    A To-Do List for the New Year *(January 2010)*
    A New List for a New Year *(January 2011)*
    Dietary Resolutions *(January 2012)*
    Do Over *(January 2014)*
    What a Colorful World *(January 2016)*

Winter Lingers 15
    Bidding Winter Adieu *(March 2010)*
    The Quiet Month *(January 2013)*
    Got Milk? Got Bread? *(February 2013)*
    A Few of My Favorite Things *(December 2014)*
    Snowflakes and Snowfalls *(January 2015)*

Settled in New Surroundings 25
    Count Me In *(April 2010)*
    Degrees of Separation *(August 2010)*
    Landing in Farmville *(July 2014)*
    For Auld Lange Syne *(February 2015)*
    Collecting Art *(October 2015)*

Meeting New People 35
    Another Road to Farmville *(October 2010)*
    A Piece of Heaven *(May 2012)*
    A Dream Fulfilled *(September 2014)*
    Newly Planted *(May 2015)*

Currently Reading 43
Check It Out *(October 2009)*
Curling Up with a Good Book *(February 2011)*
Read Anything Good Lately? *(February 2012)*
Farmville's Literary Landscape *(February 2014)*
Winter Reading Recommendations *(February 2016)*

Feathered Friends 53
For the Birds *(February 2010)*
Humming Along *(July 2010)*
The Sounds of Morning *(May 2013)*
I'm a Birdwatcher *(June 2014)*
Rooting for the Ravens *(April 2016)*

Four-Legged Fauna 63
Why Did the Turtle Cross the Road? *(May 2011)*
Mooooving Along *(October 2012)*
On the Nature of Mice *(June 2013)*
Baffled *(October 2013)*
Lying Down on the Job *(March 2015)*

Going Buggy 73
Flutter By *(April 2012)*
Beloved Bees *(March 2016)*
Twinkle, Twinkle, Little Bug *(June 2016)*

Caring for the Yard and the World 79
Snake in the Grass *(September 2010)*
A Field of Trees *(March 2011)*
Harvest Time *(September 2011)*
Getting the Worm *(June 2015)*
Be a Superhero *(July 2015)*

Around Town 89
Happy Trails to You *(June 2010)*
What's On TV Tonight? *(April 2011)*
Not "Nothing to Do" *(October 2011)*
For the First Time *(March 2012)*
My Journey of a Thousand Miles *(May 2014)*
Into the Future *(May 2016)*

Discovering Connections 101
Better Education *(November 2011)*
Has It Been Such a Long Time? *(August 2013)*
Learning the Lingo *(April 2014)*
Urban vs. Rural Living *(October 2014)*
Farmville, That's Where I Live *(August 2015)*

The Stars Above 111
Natural Treasures in the Sky Overhead *(September 2009)*
A Different Kind of History *(May 2010)*
Once in a Blue Moon *(August 2012)*
Hope Rewarded *(November 2014)*

Sharing the Night Sky 121
Starry, Starry Night... Or Not *(July 2011)*
The Comets Are Coming *(March 2013)*
Plan B *(March 2014)*
Finding North *(April 2015)*
A Blood-Red Super Harvest Moon *(September 2015)*

Summers and Vacations 131
It's Good to Be Back Home Again *(June 2012)*
Seeing Stars *(July 2012)*
In a Hurry *(April 2013)*
I'd Rather Be *(July 2013)*
Going Down *(August 2014)*
Summertime Tasks *(July 2016)*

In God's Hands 143

Not the End *(June 2011)*
The Churches of Farmville *(August 2011)*
Beside Still Water *(September 2012)*

Colder Days and Warmer Hearts 149

Falling in Love with Fall *(November 2009)*
Worth Getting Up For *(November 2010)*
Applesauce! *(November 2012)*
The Seasonal Clock Strikes Autumn *(September 2013)*
Kids These Days *(November 2013)*

Christmas Time 159

Traditions Worth Keeping *(December 2009)*
Reflections *(December 2010)*
Such a Small Thing *(December 2011)*
At the Calendar's End *(December 2012)*
Sending Seasonal Greetings *(December 2013)*
The Star of Bethlehem *(December 2015)*

Postlude 171

Still Happy, Grateful Too *(November 2015)*

HAPPY TO BE HERE

Prelude

WHY FARMVILLE
August 2009

"Why Farmville? I mean, how did you even find it?"

We moved to Farmville from Michigan a few months ago. Everyone we've met has asked this. Verbatim. It's like a community script.

If we had arrived to work at Longwood University or Hampden-Sydney College, our choice might be viewed as logical. But we didn't. We have a small, home-based business and the freedom to take it wherever we want. All we need is a phone line and an internet connection. And, yes, out of the entire country (globe, for that matter) we picked Farmville.

Our decision-making process began in late February of 2004 at 2:00 a.m. Let me describe the scene: At that bleak hour, our youngest child needed to be delivered to the high school because his band was going on a trip. Our older children were both away at college. For the first time in two decades we were being set free from the day-to-day duties of parenthood.

You also need to understand that in Michigan in February, the snow on the ground has been there for months. Gritty, grimy, and grey. Not Christmas card snow. Temperatures are still below freezing, and the sun has been mostly behind clouds since Thanksgiving. Spring is nearly three months away.

So, when my husband asked what I wanted to do to celebrate our reprieve, I said I wanted to go out to dinner—as far south as we could get by driving straight through until dinner time. After consulting the map, we figured we could get to Raleigh, North Carolina.

HAPPY TO BE HERE

In late February that year, Raleigh was beginning to bloom. We enjoyed a wonderful dinner, went to a play, and spent the weekend driving around the countryside. Daffodils. Not a snowbank in sight. A seed was planted. Someday, we assured each other, we're going to move south.

Many people in Michigan who "move south" head to Florida or Arizona. But, even though we wanted a more moderate winter, we did still hope to enjoy all four seasons. After all, how does one appreciate the full wonder of spring without enduring at least something of winter? And, although Raleigh is a wonderful place to visit, we really hoped for a less urban setting. As the years moved forward, we spent time traveling through and around the southeast, always keeping a watchful eye for the perfect spot.

One spring, we stayed at a bed and breakfast in Clarksville. The owner listened to our story and suggested that we check out a town called Farmville. "Just go straight up Route 15," she said. "You can't miss it."

And that's how we found Farmville. It's straight up Route 15. You can't miss it.

But why did we choose it? The people of Farmville made us feel welcome. The desk clerks and other workers at the hotel we frequented always greeted us kindly. The coffee shop baristas made wonderful lattes and provided tips about local events. We discovered High Bridge Trail State Park, attended the community theater, went to the movies, and enjoyed the restaurants. We felt like we belonged.

Long-time residents can still be perplexed as to why this all seemed perfect to us. They are quick to point out that Farmville is just a small town in the middle of ... well, nowhere. They explain that it's an hour's drive to get anywhere.

But we see it differently. Farmville is a treasure. It's a small enough place that we encounter our new neighbors and recently made friends every time we venture out, but it's a big enough place to offer a vast array of social opportunities and an incredibly diverse cultural life. Already we've had to miss out on some events because there were too many things from which to choose.

And if we want something that Farmville doesn't offer... Well, it's only an hour's drive to almost everything.

A TO-DO LIST FOR THE NEW YEAR

January 2010

Years ago, after recognizing their futility, I gave up on New Year's resolutions. But that doesn't mean that I don't have hopes and aspirations. This year, my goal is to make headway in the process of adjusting to our new surroundings. To help accomplish this, I've made a "to do" list of nine specific things that I think will help me achieve a truer sense of belonging in the Farmville community.

1. *Learn how to pronounce it.* Farmville. Is it two equal syllables, "Farm" plus "ville" or an accented "Farm" followed by a more indistinct "vull"? I hear it both ways, so apparently I'm not the only one who is confused.

2. *Find the slot machines.* If the correct pronunciation is—as some insist—Farm Vegas, there must be slot machines somewhere. So far the closest thing I've seen is a gas station selling lottery tickets.

3. *Drive down the middle of the road.* At first, I thought the community hosted a large European population with people who had trouble remembering which side of the road the crazy Americans preferred. Then, I discovered that the habit of straddling the center line is simply a local sport designed to help keep up the excitement on blind curves. I haven't yet summoned the courage to try.

4. *Identify "the" country.* The good old U. S. of A., our nation, is "a" country, but it's not "the" country. When people first talked of "the" country, I assumed they meant a sort of pastoral, rural setting. Apparently the

definition is more precise than that. For example, I can sit on my porch and listen to cows down the street mooing, but because I can also get to the post office in five minutes, I'm not in "the" country. There must be an official boundary. Some pleasant Sunday afternoon I'm going to go look for it.

5. *Find a parking space for attending events at Longwood University.* I have enjoyed several events at Longwood, including lectures and even an opera. But I don't live in a dorm, and I don't have parking privileges, so such ventures typically culminate in a hike around town as I try to remember where I left my car. Moonlight and gentle wafting breezes can turn the search into a romantic walk, but sheets of monsoon-quality rain create an entirely different ambiance.

6. *Speaking of downpours, I need to find out who is in charge of building the ark.* According to weather statistics, since I moved here there have been 94 days of rain. This is more than double the 40 days that launched Noah. Prudence seems to dictate that I get ark tickets before they are sold out.

7. *Make a list of nasty things to say about deer.* I'm grateful for digital photography, which allows me to snap as many pictures of the deer who venture into my yard as I want without paying for developing. But I've learned that some folk around here don't want to listen to me talk about how beautiful the deer are or describe the twin fawns I watched all last summer. Instead, they want to know if my husband has come up with any unique ways to run them off.

8. *Find out what a Hokie is.* I know the orange and maroon markings identify it with Virginia Tech, but no one has been able to tell me what kind of beast it represents. A common bumper sticker seems to suggest that a Hokie may be some sort of chicken, but so far, I haven't found any taxonomic evidence.

9. *Create a "Farmville Legacy Map."* History abounds in Farmville, and many instructions on how to find places include references to years past, like "It's in the old pharmacy building." Or, my favorite, "You can't miss it. Just turn at the corner where the theater used to be." Sorry, friend, apparently I did miss it—by several years. But I thank you in advance for being patient with me as I work to understand the layers of history that make this place so special, the contemporary vitality that enriches it, and how to find my place in it all.

A NEW LIST FOR A NEW YEAR
January 2011

Last January I presented you with a list of things I hoped to accomplish during 2010. I'm pleased to report that I didn't do too badly.

I located "where the old theater used to be" (the corner of Main Street and Fourth Street; current home of the Crute Stage), and I found the borders of "the country" (far enough out of town that you have to take the family car—or, more likely, truck—to visit your closest neighbor). I even learned that a Hokie is a fearsome fighting fowl and is certainly not a chicken.

But, I didn't get everything done. My goals had been focused on learning to fit into the community, and to accomplish this I thought I'd need to participate in the local sport of straddling the center line while driving around blind curves on narrow, shoulderless roads. Well, a Hokie may not be a chicken, but I sure am. I get all the adrenaline rushes and heart pumping scares I can handle just from oncoming traffic already skilled at this game. I'm taking this undone task off my to-do list.

Accomplishing the objectives on my list was also affected by changing weather patterns. At the time I compiled last year's goals, we'd had so much rain, I was concerned about securing space on the ark. I even tried rounding up some animals, two by two, but never managed to assemble more than a pair of squirrels who were—and still are—content to wait at my bird feeder. When the summer brought drought, I realized I'd be a better neighbor if I abandoned ark preparations in favor of rain dancing classes.

After considering last year's failures and successes, I thought it appropriate to turn my attention toward the things I'd like to accomplish in 2011:

1. *Watch the sun set over Briery Creek Lake.* One day last year, I did get a chance to walk around the boat landing area, soak up the peace in the gentle breeze, and watch fish dart around submerged tree trunks.

But I had to leave before sunset, and I bet it was magnificent. This year, I'm going to plan better.

2. *Visit the Longwood Center for the Visual Arts.* The LCVA is housed in a building right at the corner of Main Street and Third Street. I've walked past it dozens of times, but I've never walked through the entrance. So to the LCVA staff, please hold the door, I'm on my way.

3. *Try my hand at kayaking.* My past experience with watercraft primarily involves cruise ships. I'm really good at deck lounging and fine dining, but my budget doesn't permit more than an occasional indulgence. I thought kayaking might be the next best thing. I missed the day these were demonstrated on Wilck's Lake last year, and I'm hopeful that a similar opportunity will present itself this year.

4. *Attend a football game at Hampden-Sydney College.* When it comes to sports, I have a hard time remembering which teams play football and which ones play baseball or hockey. But, I do know that the goal of football involves goal posts. I also understand there's no excitement like the thrill of rooting for the home team. Go Tigers! One of these days, I'll be there to cheer you on.

5. *Plant a tomato.* With all the fields and growing things in the surrounding countryside, my thumbs are starting to get itchy to try some agriculture of my own. I understand the basic rule of gardening is that if I plant it, the deer will eat it. But, I was inspired during the past growing season by pictures of roof-top tomatoes. I wondered if I could devise an equally ingenious way to outsmart these four-footed friends. If I can manage to protect a single tomato this year, maybe an entire garden could be in my future.

So although I haven't yet figured out whether local people are properly called "Farmvillains" or "Farmvillites," I have discovered the joy of making community connections, and I'm looking forward to growing deeper roots in the year to come.

DIETARY RESOLUTIONS
January 2012

Last January, I described things I planned to do during 2011—grow tomatoes, go to a Hampden-Sydney football game, and so on. My list included experiences that would help me cultivate deeper roots and become more firmly established in Farmville and the life of the surrounding community.

By September, I had accomplished only two of my goals. I knew I needed to buckle down and focus. The year evaporated, and it was the very last week before I checked off my final two items—a visit to the Longwood Center for the Visual Arts and a stop at Briery Creek Lake at sunset. So, while it was a squeaker, I did in fact accomplish everything I planned for myself in 2011.

My process of trying to become a more authentic Farmvillite has hit a snag, however. One specific boundary threatens to forever identify me as a transplant. The trouble shows up at dinner when traditional food items are discussed, often with glee. Despite my best attempts to keep a neutral expression, my nose wrinkles, my face turns green, and I am marked as alien.

As a result, this year I have decided to join the scores of people who make dietary resolutions for the new year. I understand that these decisions demonstrate my lack of an adventurous spirit in the kitchen; nevertheless, I feel firm in these resolves:

1. *I will not eat pig feet.* I've been informed that these are called "trotters" and that they are especially fine when pickled. I'm sorry, but I agree with another transplant to the area who commented: "I know where they've been."

2. *Despite the fact that brains originate in the opposite end of the animal, I'm afraid I won't be eating them either.* I've been assured that brains are good scrambled with eggs. I've always understood "scrambled brains" as a metaphor for confusion rather than as a breakfast item. I think I'll keep it that way.

3. *A third thing I plan to avoid is chitlins.* When I first heard of this dish, it seemed intriguing. The word itself has a rather happy, crunchy sort of sound. Unfortunately, it turns out that chitlins are really pig intestines. My gastronomic reflexes have been fully programmed to protect me from such things.

4. *Tripe is another thing that I hope will not appear on my table.* In an abstract sense, the word means something worthless and possibly offensive. In the literal, culinary sense, however, tripe is stomach. My taste buds imagine that there is probably a reason the word evolved this duality of meaning, and I'm content to rely on the judgement of my linguistic forbearers.

5. *I do not plan to try squirrel.* We nearly had a chance for squirrel barbecue at Christmas time when one of our backyard residents chewed through the wire on a strand of outdoor Christmas lights. The squirrel survived; the lights did not. I've been told that squirrels taste like chicken. If I want something that tastes like chicken, I'll order chicken. And, despite the incident with the lights, I've grown rather fond of our squirrels. Eating one would seem like eating a pet.

6. *I'm also going to avoid oysters.* I've heard stories about how oysters were considered a delicacy, and their arrival at one of the regional train stations was eagerly awaited. While my dislike of some other dishes is based entirely on unfounded prejudice, my decision to avoid eating oysters comes from experience. I have tasted oyster. Baked, boiled, fried, stewed, and on the half shell. My conclusion is that oysters are good for only one thing: Pearls. And that's not the part people eat.

In the spirit of compromise I may be willing to try okra or greens. I may even be willing to try Brunswick stew. When it comes to organs and animals that set off my internal squeamish alarms, however, I'm afraid I'll always carry the mark of a transplant. But, I'm pleased to report that this particular transplant is taking root rather nicely.

DO OVER
January 2014

During a visit last year, one of my sons tried to teach me how to play a game called "Go." It's an ancient Asian game that has been played for thousands of years. The game's history stretches back a millennium longer than the antecedents of chess.

The Go board is a simple grid of intersecting lines, like a sheet of graph paper. Players use pieces called stones. In the distant past, I assume players used actual stones. My son's game board uses pieces that look like black and white M&Ms. Go's primary goals are to define and protect a territory and to capture your opponent's pieces, but during the game it is also fun to watch patterns emerge as the stones are played.

In trying to take part in the game, I made a lot of mistakes. I often mistook which lines were directly connected, a seemingly simple concept but somehow visually complicated (at least to me). I looked toward distant goals and in the process missed immediate perils. Or, I defended against imminent threats and failed to consider the longer term consequences.

My son graciously pointed out my major blunders and repeatedly gave me chances to take back my stones and try to make a better play. According to the rules, he had every right to pounce on my errors and lay claim to my pieces. But he didn't, and because of that I think we both had more fun. In addition, the safe arena for practicing helped me learn to be a better player. I'm looking forward to an opportunity to try again. I have high hopes that the experience I gained will help me better handle a future challenge. Maybe next time, I'll even win a round.

Celebrating the arrival of a new year seems to bring a similar spirit of optimism. Taking down the old calendar and hanging a new one offers 365 chances to try again. It's a time to pause and recall moments that went badly, to think about how I might do things differently the next time, and also to remember things that went well and plan to repeat them.

Perhaps it's not surprising that so many diverse cultures around the world, even those that mark the beginning of a new year at different seasons, embrace the concept of starting over. Roman Catholic and Protestant Christians who follow a liturgical calendar start their year off with a season called Advent. It encompasses the four weeks before Christmas, and people are encouraged to seek forgiveness so that they can move forward with a clean slate. The Islamic year begins with a month during which people also repent of past wrongs and resolve to do better in the future. Among some Japanese Buddhist communities, the new year ceremony involves ringing a bell to drive away impure desires. A Chinese festival welcomes the new year with traditions that honor the past and look toward prosperity in the future.

The Gregorian calendar that governs our everyday life begins each year with January, a month named for the Roman god Janus. His mythological duties included watching over passageways, transitions, and new beginnings. Janus had two faces and was famous for looking back into the past while gazing forward into the future. Under his watchful eye, we start the year with renewed opportunities—not merely the chance to repeat actions but the possibility of facing similar challenges and making better moves.

This power to look back and learn from experience and the capacity to look forward with hope depend on something remarkably similar to the ability to receive and give forgiveness. I have noticed that when I make a blunder and trespass against someone or when they misstep and violate something of mine, we have choices to make. We can pounce on each other and demand retribution, or we can let the offending party take it back and try again. Forgiving and being forgiven enhance relationships and provide the means by which we all can become better people, better players in a pastime even older than Go. It's called life.

WHAT A COLORFUL WORLD
January 2016

Isn't the world supposed to be drab and monochromatic this time of year? Trees stretch out bare branches. Flowers wait for brighter days. Night lingers, and darkness renders the world in shades of grey.

Yet, I've recently observed some spectacular displays of color. On a crispy morning a few weeks ago, I watched the sun rise over a frosty field. It filled the entire eastern sky with streaks of brilliant salmon and purple. Several days later, a series of sunsets featured deep crimson and glowing orange. On an overcast day, I watched a vividly red cardinal sitting on an evergreen branch. And not long ago while I was walking on a sunny day, a small yellow dandelion caught me by surprise when it peeked out from under a brown oak leaf.

Human touches add a splash to nature's colors. The Christmas season sported multicolored lights. Advertisers displayed flamboyant choices from an entire palate of options. And now as colder days approach, people wrap themselves in sweaters and scarves of plaids and stripes.

These unexpected colors lend an air of optimism to the start of a new year. The Louis Armstrong classic "What a Wonderful World," (written by Bob Thiele and first recorded in 1967), has been on my mind. It's a hopeful song, and I've been noticing how much it uses color to convey its positive outlook. Green trees. Red roses. Blue skies. White clouds. Even a rainbow.

The emphasis of those particular colors resonates with how our eyes work and with important cultural symbols.

The human eye has red, green, and blue photoreceptors that react to lightwaves in the visible portion of the electromagnetic spectrum. The actual perception of color occurs in the brain, and all the colors the human eye sees result from mixing red, green, and blue light in various proportions. If you've got a computer monitor or television, you may already be familiar with how colors can be created using percentages of red, green, and blue. White light results from combining all three colors. If you omit one, or even if you get them out of balance, you see a different color, not white. To get a rainbow, you start with white light and separate it into its constituent parts. Isaac Newton demonstrated this during the late seventeenth century in experiments using a prism.

Getting back to the imagery in Louis Armstrong's song, tree leaves appear green because human eyes perceive the wavelengths of the light they reflect as green. Chlorophyll in the leaves absorbs light at other wavelengths for use in the process of photosynthesis. Red flowers reflect the wavelengths we perceive as red. The sky is blue because the chemical composition of earth's atmosphere scatters blue wavelengths of light more efficiently than the other wavelengths. As a result, those are the photons that that enter our eyes.

But what do the colors mean? Different cultures have different perspectives, and most colors carry more than one connotation. Within the context of Armstrong's song, it seems to me that green symbolizes life and growth. Red stands for love and passion. Blue reminds us of loyalty and faithfulness. Combine them and you get white, signifying purity, innocence, and virtue. The colors of the rainbow suggest the diversity of the human family.

It seems somewhat ironic that white—a color often associated with concepts such as goodness, incorruptibility, and even piety—cannot be created by any single wavelength of light standing alone. Although the color white carries the inference of being unadulterated, uncontaminated, and unpolluted, its attributes can be created only when dissimilar segments blend together in harmony. Pure white requires all of its constituent components or it isn't pure. If a color intended as white omits any of its red, blue, or green, the hue becomes tainted, tinted, and impure.

And that leads me to my wishes for the new year. My hope for the coming year is that we will find it within our grasp to fashion a wonderful, colorful world where we all shine together.

BIDDING WINTER ADIEU
March 2010

People often ask me if the winter we've just endured is like the winters I experienced in southeast Michigan. The answer is a complicated mix of partly yes but mostly no.

In terms of temperature and sunshine, this winter has been quite different. Just a couple weeks ago, one person complained that there hadn't been a day in the 70s since last November. I was stunned. Was there supposed to be?

I agree that it has indeed been cold—we have had three days when, even during the warmest part of the day, the temperature didn't get above freezing. This seems to be colder than average for this part of the country and certainly colder than I expected—but not colder than what I was used to. In the Detroit area so far this winter, there have been 47 days where high temperatures failed to get above freezing, including one stretch of 13 consecutive days in early January where the temperatures stayed below freezing all the time. This is actually fairly average for there. Furthermore, in the Detroit area, there has been just one clear, sunny day in the last three months and only 20 days on which the sun peeked out from behind the clouds at all. Here, we've seen the sun at least part of the time on 50 days.

But the big question is about how much snow has fallen. Using some of the tools available at Weather Underground (http://www.wunderground.com)—my favorite online spot for weather-related information—I found an interesting coincidence: As of February 13, 2010, Richmond International Airport had accumulated a total seasonal snowfall of 27.5 inches. On the very same day, the total seasonal snowfall recorded at Detroit Metropolitan Airport was identical, exactly 27.5 inches. Since then, the Richmond total has remained pretty much the same, but the Detroit numbers have continued to creep up. A snowstorm during the last week of February brought their total to 40 inches—not much more than the area's average and well below the nearly 60 inches they saw last year.

The relationship between actual snowfall and annual averages explains why this year's seemingly similar amounts of snow are really profoundly different. In Michigan, this year's snowfall has been "business as usual." Around here, we set records. Record-breaking snow has advantages over normal snow. Although it creates a hardship, it is the kind of hardship that solidifies the bonds between those who endure it together. I was proud to see how my neighbors helped one another and how the entire community made adjustments for the unusual conditions. Twenty years from now, when I'm sitting with friends reminiscing, I'll be proud to say, yes, I remember the winter of 09–10. While I hope we don't repeat it, I'm glad I didn't miss it.

Perhaps the biggest difference between the winters in both areas, however, is that winter here is essentially over. Spring is on the calendar for this month, and most folks expect it to arrive on schedule. Signs are already evident. The robins and bluebirds are back. The sun lingers in the sky until at least dinnertime. Motorcycles and bicycles can be seen around town. Kids on the college campuses sport T-shirts. In Michigan, the calendar will say spring, but most folks won't start looking for it for another month or two.

People who ask my husband and me about the weather seem to fall into two categories. Some assure us that the harsh, stormy season we've just endured is the weather's attempt to make us feel welcome. It's an odd version of that famous southern hospitality. Others, however, jest that the bad weather is our fault. They suggest that we brought it with us or somehow summoned it. In case there is any validity to this point of view, my husband is investigating the possibility of a career change. He figures there's probably a lot of money to be made as a weather god. I just wish he were as good with mild balmy breezes as he apparently is with blizzards.

… WINTER LINGERS

THE QUIET MONTH
January 2013

Our house is newly quiet. Or, I suppose it would be more accurate to say, it is quiet again. My usual mode, especially during my working hours, is to enfold myself in the kind of silent stillness that lets thoughts be heard. My normal practice is to work without the background drone of a television or radio. The quiet is interrupted only by occasional spurts of activity from domestic machinery: The furnace clicks on. The coffee pot gurgles. The dryer buzzer announces that another load is ready to be folded. Occasionally, I hear my husband walk from one room to another or up the stairs.

In the spring, summer, and autumn months, I may open a window and indulge in nature's sounds—the breeze in the trees, the chattering of squirrels, the symphony of birds. I especially love to hear falling rain or the distant rumble of thunder. But January's quiet is of a different sort. It feels deeper and stiller. And it carries with it a more profound sense of rest.

Perhaps this is because the days are still short and the quiet comes with early darkness. Or, perhaps it is simply because it contrasts so sharply with the preceding holidays.

During the most recent Christmas season, our house was filled with extra footsteps, voices, and music. My children stacked CDs in the player beginning with familiar holiday songs, shifting to newer renditions sung by people and bands I'd never heard of before, and finally drifting into an eclectic mix that ranged from Glenn Miller to electronica. Siblings toting opposing laptop computers shared online videos and their favorite silly pictures of cats. (Question: Why are there so many funny pictures of cats on the internet? Answer: Because dog owners actually go outside sometimes.) Laughter bounced off our walls. "Remember when" stories circled the living room.

A contemporary addition to the holiday sound track emerged from the combined tones of the assembled cell phones. One sounded like an old-fashioned telephone ring, but most were snippets of tunes or various gongs. The biggest attention-getter consisted of beeps, burbles, and squeals in the voice of R2D2 of Star Wars fame.

At night, when everyone was sleeping, I thought I heard angels dancing on our roof.

Back in the kitchen, a mixer that usually lies dormant emerged to work on traditional holiday fare. Dishes clinked and cupboards creaked. The refrigerator door groaned as it got more than its accustomed amount of exercise, and the oven timer kept us all synchronized.

When I asked one of my sons to "run upstairs and call your father to dinner," he pounded up the stairs, did an immediate U-turn, and sprinted back down. I started to question the seemingly forgotten "call your father to dinner" part of the request. Before I could put the query into words, he pulled his cell phone from his pocket and quite literally complied with my request.

But now they're gone. They've returned to their adult places in the world, and the rush of noise that momentarily coalesced under our roof has been muted by distance. We've resumed the more sedate practice of talking by e-mail, and the only ring tone that breaks into my routine belongs to my own phone.

As much as I enjoyed the commotion—and even miss it—I find myself now prepared for January's more serene days and elongated nights. Lingering momentarily here in the midst of winter's hush, I'm enjoying the calm, the softness and warmth of sweatshirts and blankets, and the tranquility of starlight. I feel content as life's seasons ebb and flow, and I'm thankful for this brief time of respite. The new year has arrived, but it hasn't yet revealed what it will be. Its deadlines, challenges, and stresses are still a mystery. Its accomplishments, thrills, and joys are waiting to be discovered.

I know the days are already growing longer, and I know I'll soon be looking for signs of spring. But for these few moments in the quiet of January, I am at peace.

GOT MILK? GOT BREAD?
February 2013

When my husband and I moved to Farmville, one of our neighbors explained local winter preparedness customs. "If there's so much as the hint of a snowflake in the forecast," she explained, "everyone rushes to the store to buy milk and bread. Those shelves will be picked clean." We smiled, maybe we smirked.

At the time, we were still winter snobs—the kind of people who dismissed subfreezing temperatures as merely "normal" for winter and laughed when people worried about the cold and a bit of snow.

During our first winter in Farmville, I attended an evening event at Hampden-Sydney College. Although the day had been bright and clear, as the sun set, the mercury in the thermometer descended with it. Temperatures dipped below 60 and threatened to continue falling. Anticipating a possible chill, I put on my sweater and headed out.

We joined the crowd assembling in Crawley Auditorium. A gentleman came in and took the seat at the end of our row. He wore a handsome wool coat and had a scarf wrapped around his neck. As he sat down, he removed a hat and peeled a pair of gloves from his hands. I poked my husband in the side and remarked, "Some people must think it's cold."

I may have shed my sweater. I was still caught in the clutches of a different climate.

Moving forward a few years, I confess I have discovered how quickly a person can adapt to a new reality. Now I find myself looking for a sweater if temperatures fall below 70. Below 60, means I need to grab my jacket. Below 50, and I'm the one with my wool coat buttoned up to my ears. Last Christmas I even asked for—and received—a warm scarf and matching gloves.

Some of my other winter habits have also changed. During that first winter, I developed the annoying hobby of chatting with people in colder regions and casually asking about their weather. "Oh, is it really only 18 degrees there? Gosh, it's sort of cold here, too. They're saying that the temperature may fall into the 40s later in the week." Snicker. Chortle.

Recently, however, I seem to have metamorphosed into a target for people who live farther south. Friends and family in Florida ask me, "How's your weather?" They want to hear me shiver. They want me to regale them with stories about being able to see my breath or having to scrape frost from my windshield. They especially want to hear about cancelled events and other inconveniences related to snow and traffic hazards. After listening to the particulars, they'll say something like, "I was out on the boat yesterday. It was 80." I hear muffled giggles.

I do still perform the same stunt with people in colder climates, but now it's completely inadvertent. For example, a few weeks ago I complained to my daughter about our three inches of snow and temperatures that threatened to fall below freezing at night. I wasn't trying to taunt her. I was simply miffed that Mother Nature had decided to throw a bit of winter my way. In that state of mind, I momentarily forgot that my daughter was dealing with an entirely different reality in Colorado. "Try this on for size," she retorted. "Minus 16, minus 17. The other day it got up to a balmy positive 12 degrees."

Then, I realized that living in south central Virginia had adjusted my notion of normal. Suddenly our frigid winter felt fairly mild, and I stopped being amused by the hardships others were enduring.

But although the reminder that winters were much harsher in other places helped me refocus, that awareness didn't give me any immunity against developing an obsession with milk and bread. Just the other day, I peeked ahead at the five-day forecast and noticed the possibility of more snow. An urgent need to go to the store and buy milk and bread immediately sprouted within me. Apparently the compulsion is contagious, and I've got a confirmed case. I've also got milk and bread.

A FEW OF MY FAVORITE THINGS
December 2014

Many of my favorite things are associated with warmer seasons: riding my bike in the sun, walking on the warm sand of a beach, catching the scent of flowers in the air, watching butterflies and hummingbirds. I could go on and on.

Then winter approaches. Over the years, I have developed a bad habit of reflexively dreading the things I don't like about the winter months. Icy walkways, snow-covered roads, cold hands and chapped lips, heating bills. But I can't go on and on. In fact, while taking a recent inventory on the subject, I was surprised to realize how many pieces of winter are actually among my favorite things.

First, there is the growing darkness that fortifies the night sky. As nights lengthen during late fall, the constellation Orion swings up over the eastern horizon. The mythical hunter lofts his club and grips his shield as he wards off Taurus the bull. His sword hangs from his famous belt. The Pleiades, a tight cluster also known as the Seven Sisters, rides on the bull's back. Orion's faithful hunting dogs mount into the sky behind him. Sirius, known as the Dog Star, appears as the brightest of all the night's stars, and sometimes when the atmospheric conditions are just right, it twinkles in disco fashion, flashing blue, red, green, and white. Crispy cold nights with their low humidity offer a perfect opportunity to see the stars with an intensity that summer's haze often blurs.

Then there are my favorite sweaters, sweatshirts, scarf, and coat. I currently own two sweaters that I especially enjoy because of how they embrace me in fluffy softness—a sensory version of tranquility. As much as I love my sweaters, I don't get a chance to enjoy them for months at a stretch when summer's temperatures reach into the 80s and 90s. As soon as the thermometer starts to flirt with the freezing mark, however, I'm wrapped from head to toe in soft serenity.

Cold days also provide the perfect motivation for making homemade soup and filling my kitchen with the aroma of baking. During the heat of summer, I'm often loath to make dinners that require turning the stove or oven on for very long. Winter days are different. When it's cold out, I'm eager to let the kettle simmer for hours and keep the oven busy with breads, casseroles, and cookies.

The winter smells of a kitchen hard at work remind me of other things I like to do indoors—ferreting out patterns embedded in a Sudoku puzzle, family rivalries over a cribbage board, watching an old movie, or curling up with a good book. I bought a bag of books during the autumn sale sponsored by the Friends of the Farmville-Prince Edward Community Library. I'll need an ample number of sufficiently cold days during the winter months if I'm going to finish them before warmer days lure me back outside.

And, of course, the arrival of winter ushers in another holiday season. Christmas lights brighten our neighborhoods. Festive decorations spread good cheer. Mugs of hot cider and cocoa warm hearts and hands. In churches, people gather to sing special hymns, and the air fills with wonder. Here in Farmville, the Waterworks players present their Christmas pantomime, and the High Bridge Railroad Club opens its doors so everyone can relive the fun of watching model trains chug past miniature scenery along elaborate systems of tracks.

Although it's tempting to dwell on winter's negative aspects—I still dislike driving in snow and I worry about people who don't have adequate food or shelter from the cold—this year I'm trying to remember that winter also offers many delights. And I need to enjoy them now. Lengthening days will soon restrict the number of hours available for stargazing. Rising temperatures will send my sweaters to the back of the closet. I'll hang up my apron, and my soup kettle will get pushed to the rear of the cupboard. In just a few short months, this wonderful winter will be gone.

SNOWFLAKES AND SNOWFALLS
January 2015

Snowflakes have been on my mind since the *The Farmville Herald* began collecting entries in its annual contest to predict when the first measurable snowfall would occur. Not if, but when. By the time you read this, perhaps some snowy days will have arrived, but as I'm writing these words, this season hasn't yet produced a measurable snowfall, at least locally. I didn't enter the contest, but its existence made me sufficiently curious to do some weather-related research.

According to National Weather Service records spanning the last thirty years of the twentieth century, Richmond annually experiences 6.3 days of snowfall with a total accumulation of 11.9 inches. (Richmond is the closest location for which I could find detailed data.) The days that typically receive snow include one in December, two in January, two in February, and one in March.

Another weather chart based on data spanning the years from 1898 to 2005 is also pertinent to *The Herald's* contest. It shows the percent chance of measurable snowfall on specific days throughout the winter. The first spike in likelihood, representing a 10% chance it will snow on a specific date, occurs in mid-December. There are three more spikes in January: a 12% chance at mid-month, another 12% chance about a week before the end of the month, and a 14% chance as the last day of January approaches. The day associated with the largest percent chance of a snowfall measuring at least four inches occurs just past mid-February, but it precedes a few days when the likelihood of getting any snow at all plunges briefly to a mere 4%.

Although these statistics are interesting, the tale of how flakes are formed reveals the true beauty of snow. Each snowflake is individually crafted by its surroundings. Here's how it works: Air in the environment contains water vapor and tiny bits of dust and pollen. When it gets extremely cold, water droplets freeze onto the particles. Ice crystals develop. Ice crystals form in hexagonal shapes because of the way water molecules are structured. As more water vapor freezes onto a crystal, arms begin to sprout from each of its six corners. A snowflake is born.

Environmental conditions influence how the flake will develop. According to the National Oceanic and Atmospheric Administration, snowflakes that form at around 23 degrees Fahrenheit generally have long needle-like arms. At 5 degrees Fahrenheit, plate-like flakes are more apt to form. Humidity also plays a role. Low humidity tends to create snowflakes with simpler shapes. Higher humidity tends to lead to more complicated structures. A snowflake can encounter rapidly changing conditions as it falls or is blown around. These variations affect crystalline growth and lead to intricate and beautiful designs. Snowflakes are usually symmetrical because all six of their arms encounter atmospheric conditions that are basically alike. Tiny dissimilarities do exist, however, because there are minuscule differences in the air—even across distances no greater than the width of a snowflake. And, because no two snowflakes follow the exact same path from the cloud to the ground, each develops in a unique way. It really is true that no two snowflakes are precisely alike.

But although each individual snowflake is an unrepeatable creation, snowflakes are not the only class of objects in which every single member differs in some way from all others. We live in a culture where many items are mass produced, so it's easy to forget the uniqueness of things all around us: trees, clouds, pieces of granite, people. Even days of the year. Each moment that comes and goes is unlike any other moment that has occurred, and each moment that passes will not be repeated in exactly the same manner. Ever.

As we enter January, an entire new year's worth of days awaits. Each one will grow and unfurl in its own way, sometimes in gentle beauty and sometimes in blustering storms. Not if, but when. We will all be shaped by the days we encounter. My prayer for myself—and for you too—is that each of our distinctive designs will produce a measurable and beautiful effect on the community around us.

COUNT ME IN
April 2010

We recently passed the first anniversary of purchasing our home in Farmville, and the anniversary of our move-in date is fast approaching. At this auspicious time, it seemed especially fitting that the U.S. Census Bureau would seek to include our migration in its tally.

My census paperwork arrived along with a letter dated March 15, 2010 that encouraged me to fill out and return the form "today." I was eager to do so. But, the form asked how many people lived in my house as of April 1, 2010, and that was confusing.

My plans certainly involved living for at least a couple weeks after receiving the form, but I couldn't completely ignore the reality that my prophetic abilities are rather limited. God, in his wisdom and in accordance with his plan, can call me heavenward at any moment. He can see the end from the beginning, but I can't. It, therefore, seemed rather presumptuous to fill out such an official document in advance.

This nagged at me until a postcard arrived a week later suggesting more firmly that I should really send the census form in immediately. So I did, and I am proud to report that I have been officially counted as a Virginian.

But, while being officially numbered as a member of the community is nice, there are other unofficial signs that actually have more meaning.

Take the simple ringing of a telephone. When I first got a number with the local 434 area code, I received a lot of calls. None of them were for me. They were recorded announcements with slightly veiled intentions but obviously from collection agencies. They were looking for people with unfamiliar names. People I had never met.

It was frustrating on two accounts. First involved the sheer number of calls, including those that woke me up on weekend mornings, routinely interrupted dinner, and persisted at regular intervals throughout the day. A call would begin by saying, "This is a personal message for Jane or John Doe. If you are not Jane or John Doe, please hang up." So, I'd hang up. Only to get another call an hour later. This went on for days, weeks, months. And the calls weren't just for the one hypothetical Doe couple. There were calls for at least a dozen different names. Getting a call from a real person instead of a recorded announcement wasn't much better. Talking to a real person often meant that I had to endure some exceptionally rude treatment before being able to convince a caller that I wasn't the party they were trying to reach.

But the second reason the calls were frustrating was that none of the calls were for me. No one wanted to talk to me. It was kind of lonely.

A year later, I can report that most of those annoyance calls have dropped by the wayside. Now, my phone serves primarily to connect me with friends and businesses in the community. One recent day, a neighbor called to chat, the library called to let me know when to come help reshelve books, and a local business called to tell me an order was completed. This change in what I expect when the phone rings is certainly more a sign of belonging than simply being counted.

Another example involves going to the store. When I first moved here, it seemed that stores were filled with clusters of people greeting each other. Every time I'd turn from one aisle to another, someone would be calling out to someone. But not to me.

Not any more. Now it seems a rare excursion that I don't bump into someone and stop to chat or at least give a friendly wave. The feeling of recognizing familiar faces and being recognized counts for much more than simply being counted.

I don't know how my first year here went by so fast. A few unpacked boxes are still hiding in the closet, and already the annual inspection on my car is nearing its expiration. I still feel like the new kid, but it's official. I have been counted as one of you.

DEGREES OF SEPARATION
August 2010

A lot of people have been talking about degrees. A few months back, they meant those awarded by colleges and universities. All through July, the degrees creeping into conversations had to do with soaring triple-digit temperatures. But as I continue to meet people around town and discover connections between us, I keep thinking of degrees of separation—the notion that any two people can be connected through a chain of overlapping relationships.

The concept was voiced nearly a century ago, and then studied in the 1960s and again several decades later. Although controversial, some sociologists say the number of links in a chain between any two random individuals is apt to be surprisingly small, about six. The Disney empire captured the fundamental spirit of this claim when they sang the song, "It's a Small World."

The entertainment industry added to the fun when the actor, Kevin Bacon supposedly quipped he had worked with all the people in Hollywood (one degree of separation), or at least with someone who had worked with them (two degrees of separation). This remark resulted in the birth of a trivia game to link other actors to Bacon, finding the smallest degree of separation. Although Bacon's claim is technically not precise, a website called "The Oracle of Bacon" (that, sadly, now appears to be defunct) claimed that among actors in a database of more than a million people listed in movie credits, the average separation from Bacon was about 2.9, subject to change with every new movie.

The Farmville population is much smaller than the Oracle's database, and the corresponding connections between people seem tighter. For example, when my husband and I were in the process of buying our home, our real estate agent told us the seller was unavailable for closing during a certain week. I notified our attorney. She commented that the seller—she called him by his first name—would indeed be attending an event in another state. I don't remember which state or what event she specified, but I do recall remarking on the coincidence that two seemingly unconnected people would know so much about each other's affairs. She laughed, "Welcome to Farmville!"

Not long after we moved in, a couple we met asked where we lived. We mentioned the street name. "You must be the people who moved into…" And, they accurately identified our house. How did they know? Being friends with someone on our street, they had driven past our home several times while it was for sale.

Then recently, my husband and I were invited to a party. Mingling among unfamiliar people is not something I do with ease. I felt anxious, terrified. But, I wanted to go. I wanted to honor the hostess by joining the celebration. So, despite my internal state of panic, I accepted the invitation.

The big day arrived. At the proper time, we pulled out of our driveway. Some neighbors pulled up at a stop sign behind us. We turned left, and so did they. Through the next several turns, they remained behind us. "They're following us," my husband joked. It turned out they were headed to the same party. And, to my surprise, there were many familiar faces in the crowd. "How do you know our hostess?" I asked over and over again. Answers included clubs, church activities, working, and volunteering.

Every day I discover new, overlapping relationships that link me with others, and these connections are no trivial matter. They create the wonderful, small-town atmosphere that permeates the community. And, as a bonus, they aren't limited to here and now. They stretch deep into the past, linking people to history, and they push into the future every time a child makes a new friend.

I have heard some folk disparage the small-town environment where everyone seems to know everyone. And, I've read reports snubbing the notion of six degrees of separation between random people. Some seem to favor bigger numbers with vague, or even nonexistent, connections. But I can't help thinking that a small town has a lot to teach the world, and that a small world, where we cherished our interconnections, would be a better world.

LANDING IN FARMVILLE
July 2014

People still ask me how I happened to land in Farmville. The truth is I didn't land here at all, at least not literally. I came in on the ground via the highway system. It happened in stages that involved several trips, a car, and a rented truck. My oldest son, however, is a pilot, airplane mechanic, and flight instructor. Sometimes when he comes to visit, he flies. So although he doesn't live here, he is the member of our family who has really landed in Farmville.

My first visit to the Farmville airport occurred before I was actually a resident. My husband and I were staying at a local hotel trying to decide whether we would become Farmvillians. By a happy coincidence, our son needed to deliver a plane from the airport where he works on Long Island to a destination in Tennessee. He said, "Wow! If you're in Farmville, that's where I'm planning to stop for gas."

As it turns out, Farmville is a popular stopping point for general aviation pilots traveling up and down the east coast. General aviation means all flights that aren't commercial or military. Businesses flights, package deliveries, agricultural services, law enforcement, air ambulances, wildlife management, disaster relief, news and traffic reporting, sight-seeing, and recreational flying—they're all examples of general aviation. The Farmville airport sits in a convenient spot between Canada and Florida, and pilots know its grounds are well maintained, gas is available 24/7, and the restrooms are clean.

So we met my son at the airport and took him out to lunch. Then he accompanied us to meet with a real estate agent to look at a house. Although we didn't know it at the time, it turned out to be the one we eventually purchased.

I won't go so far as to say that the airport all by itself lured us to Farmville, but knowing that my son could occasionally stop by was certainly a perk. His visits don't happen nearly as often as I'd like (daily would suit me just fine), but every time he calls and says he's on his way, I drop whatever I'm doing and head out to the airport. I wait and watch the sky. I try to guess which arriving plane might turn out to be him.

Once while waiting, I met a couple who had flown in from Maryland. They were checking weather conditions before continuing their flight farther south. On another visit, I met a woman who was an aerobatic competitor. Pilots who serve as chauffeurs for dignitaries attending events at Longwood University and Hampden-Sydney College also sometimes hang out at the Farmville airport.

Earlier this year my son had hoped for a stopover during the week before Mother's Day. A series of misaligned weather patterns caused the trip to be cancelled. A few days later, I learned that the local Experimental Aircraft Association (EAA) chapter was hosting a Young Eagles event. Since 1992, EAA chapters across the country have given more than 1.8 million free flights to kids between the ages of 8 and 17. When my son was within the proper age range, he never missed an opportunity to take a Young Eagles ride. Because I was missing him, I thought a visit to the airport and a chance to chat with some pilots would cheer me up.

I was in for an unexpected treat. Morgan Dunnavant, an EAA member, offered me a ride in his Maule MXT-7. I didn't need any arm twisting, just a hand up and help with my seat belt. The plane lifted gently, and from an altitude of about 2000 feet, I saw my house. I saw Briery Creek in the distance, then the Sandy Creek Reservoir. I saw a stretch of High Bridge Trail State Park, and then High Bridge itself came into view. Shortly after, all of downtown unfurled.

I heard my pilot radio our approach back to the airport. We touched down and taxied back to our starting point. It wasn't until Mr. Dunnavant offered me a hand to deplane that I realized I had finally, literally landed in Farmville.

FOR AULD LANG SYNE
February 2015

Should auld acquaintance be forgot and never brought to mind? You probably associate this song with the end of the year. So, why am I singing it in February? In times long ago, the year ended with February.

The ancient Romans welcomed the new year on March 1. Sometime before the second century B.C.E., the start of the year was moved to January, the spot that is familiar to us today. But, the Latin term that gives the month its name, februum, relates to its older position. The word means "purification," and it was associated with a Roman ritual that was held during the full moon of February. It involved washing and spring cleaning in anticipation of the year to come.

I find it interesting to note that Lent, the Christian liturgical season devoted to spiritual purification by means of prayer, fasting, and penitence, begins in February (the date changes year-to-year, but it is always a Wednesday, called Ash Wednesday). During the Lenten season, Christians make a dedicated effort to recall sins, ask for forgiveness, and revitalize connections with God. These efforts help prepare believers to better labor in God's service.

This confluence of emphasis on being cleansed from the past and preparing for the future makes it seem especially fitting that February also plays host to the observance of African American History Month. In the United States, past and present treatment of African American people includes plenty for which penitence is required, and the work of moving forward is yet unfinished.

The origins of African American History Month stretch back to 1915 when Carter G. Woodson, an African American author and historian, established the Association for the Study of Negro Life and History (now known as the Association for the Study of African American Life and History). That group inaugurated the observance of Negro History Week in 1926. In 1976 during our nation's bicentennial, official recognition of February as Black History Month was given by then-president Gerald Ford. The designation has been continued by every president since that time.

Before I moved to the Farmville area, I was unaware of the community's past challenges with racial relationships and its role in shaping the national discussion regarding civil rights in education. In my ignorance, I had not known that there were places where officials closed schools rather than integrate them. Initially, I felt embarrassed to be linked to such events. I thought it would be nicer to forget that these things ever happened.

But forgetting the past does not honor the achievements of those who struggled to bring us into the future. I've since discovered that one of the brightest spots in our community sits atop the Prince Edward County Courthouse. It's called the Light of Reconciliation. The light was installed by officials in 2008. A resolution adopted at that time makes an unambiguous admission of past mistakes, confesses guilt, and expresses regret and sorrow regarding the results. Yet, the light looks to the future. The sign standing on the courthouse lawn reads in part, "When we raise our eyes to see this light, may we also incline our hearts and minds to shine our own light of reconciliation toward all people."

Thomas Perriello, who was at that time representing this region in the U.S. House of Representatives, made remarks that were officially recorded in the Congressional Record. He concluded his statement with these words: "This memorial not only looks back to the dreams deferred by locked schoolhouse doors, but also forward to a better nation, one of ever-expanding opportunity for all. Martin Luther King Jr. once said, 'Darkness cannot drive out darkness; only light can do that.' Let this light in Prince Edward County, Virginia be a permanent reminder of our ongoing struggle for a fairer world."

So, should auld acquaintance be forgot? Absolutely not. In honor of auld lang syne (the Scottish translates roughly as "days of long ago") and in full knowledge that the work is not yet complete, this February, this African American History Month, please join with me in remembering the lessons of history and the crucial need to usher in a brighter age.

COLLECTING ART
October 2015

I have a small sculpture in my office. It stands about four inches tall and consists of a twisted wire, a slice of cork, and a blue marble. I got the piece from an Art-o-mat vending machine at the Longwood Center for Visual Arts (LCVA). It was created by Farmville artist, Sandy Willcox.

The form of the sculpture intrigues me, and the various ways I interpret its meaning change based on my mood and how the sunlight hits the marble. On some days, I see myself as the marble: partly transparent, partly reflecting what goes on around me, and partly concealed. The wire, with its curls and loops, reminds me of the path my life has followed on its journey to get me where I am. The cork at the base suggests all the traditions and roots that help hold me stable. The base isn't what catches my eye, however. The entire sculpture sweeps upward, reminding me that I'm on a journey into the future, an undefined unknown.

On other days, I see the marble as the earth—a small piece of creation, a tiny ball in the vastness of a greater universe, held in its place by the principles of orbital mechanics and the law of gravity. And, like the twists in the wire that supports the marble, these forces have often demanded that physicists reconsider past assumptions and investigate evidence in a new direction. The marble humbles me when I realize how small I am in the grand scheme of things and how complicated even seemingly simple things can be.

Sometimes the wire draws my attention. I see a shape akin to a treble clef. I hear mingling strains of long-forgotten music that stir my emotions and urge me to march on. Even when I'm tired. Even when I'm weary. Even when people around me seem to be focused on a different tune.

That's a lot of meaning, especially for a tiny piece of art that came in a box the size of a cigarette pack. You see, Art-o-mat machines are repurposed cigarette vending machines. You insert payment (at LCVA the machine takes a token that costs $5), pull the knob representing the art you want, and a small box drops. Sandy is one of 400 artists whose work is available in more than 100 machines around the country. Other types of artwork include photographs, paintings, and jewelry. The scope of what's available is limited only by an artist's imagination—and the precisely defined box dimensions required for smooth vending operations. The selections change as alternate items become available, so you can make multiple visits to the machine to work on developing your very own art collection. Yet, with all the options from which to choose, my favorite is Sandy's sculpture.

Recently, I had an opportunity to enjoy more of Sandy's work. She participated in a two-person exhibition, along with her husband David Dodge Lewis, at Hampden-Sydney College's Esther Atkinson Museum. The event, "Realism: The Compelling Illusion," featured paintings by both of them. On display were works of art in which everyday objects, scenes, and portraits looked as real as photographs, but they were so much more. The images were composed to evoke deeper truths than mere realistic depiction could convey, encouraging the viewer to see an underlying reality filled—often simultaneously—with playful and poignant meanings.

David is the William W. Eliott Professor of Fine Arts at Hampden-Sydney College. His work is also featured in an exhibition titled, "The Quickening Image," which comprises dozens of drawings created through a process known as wax-resist. It features David's work along with that of Ephraim Rubenstein, who is on the faculty of the Art Students League of New York and Columbia University.

The exhibition was displayed at LCVA during the fall of 2015. After that, it hit the road to travel to other places (find it at http://www.thequickeningimage.com). But, Farmville's LCVA still has plenty to offer. If you'd like to bring some art home with you, don't miss the Art-o-mat machine. And, to learn more about two of Farmville's finest artists, David Dodge Lewis and Sandy Willcox, the next time you're online, visit Lewcox Galleries (http://www.lewcox.com).

ANOTHER ROAD TO FARMVILLE
October 2010

A reader asked if I would occasionally tell the stories of other people who have chosen to come to Farmville. I'm glad to oblige. Please allow me to introduce Roger and Linda Hamel.

Roger and Linda grew up in a farming community in New York state. Linda lived on a farm. Roger worked on his uncle's farm. They met during the fourth grade when they attended the same one-room school house. They've been a couple ever since.

Career pursuits led the Hamels to Connecticut. They made many treks back to New York and then down to Florida visiting family. On these southern drives, they always passed through Virginia. They fell in love with its pastoral landscapes, the fields, the barns and silos, and especially the horse farms with their fenced pastures. An idea took hold. "When we retire, we'd like to move to Virginia," they said to one another.

The years sped by, and as Roger's retirement approached they started to narrow their focus. Linda didn't want to go too far east, and Roger wanted to avoid the mountains. They drew a circle, centered around South Hill, with a radius of about fifty miles. For the next several years, they explored their target area.

At first, Farmville was just a town on the outer fringe of their circle. But on closer inspection, it seemed to offer the right ingredients. Linda was drawn by the friendliness of the community. "When you drive along, people wave to you. It doesn't matter if they are little or old or what color they are, they all wave," she says.

But when they looked for a place to buy, they came up empty handed. Then, about to give up, they stumbled across some property for sale. "It was 50 acres with a barn and silo and cows on it," Roger remembers. "The first time I saw it, I loved it immediately."

Linda felt warmly welcomed. "People would see our car and neighbors would stop and introduce themselves. They couldn't have been nicer. One neighbor invited us for a meal one night even though they didn't know us."

In a short time, the Hamels became immersed in the community. Roger started volunteering at Holliday Lake State Park, working so enthusiastically, the park eventually enticed him out of retirement. Now, re-retired, he has returned to volunteer roles, including his current position as President of Friends of Holliday Lake State Park. "I enjoy volunteering for the state park system," Roger says. "They're a bunch of fantastic people." The Hamels also love the parks, and they have a goal of visiting every single one. They've already been to 20, and a recently purchased camper will help them reach the remaining ones.

At home, several years ago, Roger unexpectedly unearthed a piece of history—a line of stones that turned out to be from the foundation of a 150-year-old cabin. Four Longwood classes, under the direction of Dr. James Jordan, conducted an archeological dig to learn more. Linda says they kept four mementos, but the rest of the recovered artifacts were donated to the University.

Hospitality is Linda's domain. She entertains guests from out of town, and last summer, the couple hosted a dinner for a team of girls from the Youth Conservation Corps. They served hamburgers, hotdogs, and other picnic foods, and their backyard offered a spectacular view of the fireworks at the airport.

The Hamel home also includes a woodshop where Roger makes furniture and small items. He takes special pride in one particular project. Virginia's governor came to Farmville for National Trails Day in 2009. To commemorate the occasion, the governor was given a unique set of candleholders made with glass insulators taken from old telephone poles in High Bridge Trail State Park—candleholders that Roger had expertly crafted for the occasion.

So after a decade, are they still happy to be here? Without a doubt. "For a little town, Farmville really has a lot of neat things: Heart of Virginia Festival, First Fridays, Movies Under the Stars, great restaurants, and nice shops," Linda explains. "We like the people. We have great neighbors and friends. It is a nice place."

A Piece of Heaven
May 2012

Frank and Mary Lacey came to Farmville nearly a decade ago, and they're happy to be here. Mary explains, "This is a gorgeous place. We feel like we're in a little piece of heaven." In fact, they credit divine guidance for bringing them together as a couple and leading them to make a home in Farmville.

Frank explains that he was a single man in his 40s, working as an associate pastor for a large church in the Raleigh area. That church supported a home for troubled teenage girls. Usually the workers who came to help were young women, fresh out of college. He offered up what he calls a ridiculous prayer. "I prayed that God would send someone my age to come and work with the girls."

Unbeknownst to Frank, on the opposite side of the country in Spokane, Washington, Mary had been considering her future. "I knew I was called to be involved in ministry, but I didn't know what." That's when she learned of an opportunity to work with troubled girls. "I went to be a house mom. I always knew it would be temporary, but I thought I might eventually move into administration. I didn't know I would end up as a pastor's wife!"

Mary had been on the job only a few months when she was charged with the task of formally receiving a gift of a projector on behalf of the home. Frank had the assignment of presenting the gift during a Sunday morning service. "We actually met at the altar," he laughs. They were married a year later.

Not long after, two families from Farmville who were interested in beginning a contemporary church visited the senior pastor under whom

Frank served. When the idea of starting a new church in Farmville was first mentioned to him, Frank's reaction was immediate: "No! I wouldn't even consider it. I knew Farmville. I had driven through it. It was too small."

But the issue kept coming up. Finally, Frank agreed to visit with the people in Farmville.

"It was a rainy, nasty night," he recalls. "We talked to the two couples. I was business-like and blunt. I said, 'This is the other side of the coin that you probably haven't thought about,' but they had thought about it."

As the conversation continued, Frank's eyes were opened. He thought, "These guys are awesome. Who wouldn't want to work with people like this?" His mind completely changed. Instead of not wanting to come to Farmville, he found himself eagerly thinking, "I hope they want me!"

During another visit to the area, Frank—a canoe enthusiast—discovered the Appomattox River Company. "I saw all those canoes, and I thought to myself, 'This is of God!'"

And so Riverside Community Church, an independent church affiliated with a group of relational churches under the umbrella organization ARC (Association of Related Churches), was born. The name Riverside was chosen because of its proximity to the Appomattox River and Frank's love for the water.

The church began meeting at the old cinema building, using one theater for the kids and one for the church service. When the new theater was built, the church moved along with it, and it has been moving forward ever since. Frank explains, "It took some time trying to find our niche, where we fit in the scheme of things."

"After realizing who was in our community, our focus shifted. This is an outdoor community," Mary adds, and the Laceys love being part of outdoor activities. "We like where we live, and we like where we are in life."

They hope to stay in the area for the long term. "Our dream is to retire here," Frank says. The couple's vision includes the possibility of opening a bed and breakfast or potentially hosting concerts where developing songwriters can come and polish their craft. Yet, Frank admits, "God's the boss. He'll do whatever he wants."

So whatever happens, as the coming years unfold, the Laceys are focused on the present moment, enjoying the everyday miracle of living in a heavenly place called Farmville.

A DREAM FULFILLED
September 2014

Formerly from Lynchburg, Bud and Judith Kennedy moved to Farmville in 2012. They purchased a home in this area to be closer to grandchildren. That part of their story sounds fairly typical. The route they took to get here, however, included an eight-year detour aboard a 42-foot sailboat.

When Bud served in the Navy on a ship in the Caribbean, he saw a couple living aboard a boat. He remembers thinking, "Boy, that must be the life!"

A dream was born. Then, in 1999 Bud had an encounter with prostate cancer. While recovering from surgery, he spent a lot of time looking at boats and the dream grew.

"Our brothers died of cancer," Judith explains, and she says they kept returning to the question, "Are we going to live long enough or should we just do it?"

They decided to embrace the dream. Bud says, "We went into the experience in sort of a rush. If you don't go ahead and do it you are never going to do it."

They rented out their house and went to North Carolina where they purchased a Morgan Out Island ketch. A ketch is a kind of sailboat that has two masts, a larger one in the front and a smaller one in the back. They moved onboard and learned to sail in the Pamlico Sound. After a few trial runs that included taking the intercoastal waterway to Baltimore, a trip offshore from Norfolk, and a season in the Bahamas they set out to circumnavigate the Caribbean.

For the next six years, ports with names often featured in vacation brochures became their home. Turks and Caicos Islands. The leeward and windward islands of the Lesser Antilles. Trinidad and Tobago. And a host of coastal islands and towns in countries such as Venezuela, Columbia, Panama, Honduras, and Belize.

Although the Morgan served them well, it required continual maintenance. "Nothing is easy. You can't just haul up to Jiffy Lube," Judith remarks. Once off the Columbian coast during a time of no wind, the boat's engine gave out. "We had to call the Coast Guard in Miami. They connected us with the Coast Guard in Columbia, and we were eventually towed into port."

One of their favorite places was the San Blas archipelago off the coast of Panama where they enjoyed snorkeling and getting to know the local Kuna Indians. "I swam with a spotted eagle ray," Bud says. "We saw many rays this big." He holds his arms widely outstretched. He also tells about an encounter with an octopus and recounts a story about watching a flounder move along the seafloor. He says he was looking right at it, knew exactly where it was, and yet its camouflage was so perfect, he couldn't see it when it was stationary.

Judith remembers days at sea, "There were dolphins beyond count. I could stand on the bow and the dolphins were just right there."

They both talk about the sunsets. "We've seen the green flash," Bud confides. "A couple of times," Judith adds. "Maybe even several times," Bud clarifies. The phenomenon occurs only when the atmospheric conditions are just right, and the last light rays from the setting sun (or the first rays of a rising one) are bent in a way that creates a momentary green light.

After the Kennedys returned to the U.S., they sold the boat and moved back into the home they had left behind. Nearby, builders began erecting large apartment buildings and a parking lot. They wanted peace and more space. That desire brought them to Farmville.

I asked them if they ever felt like returning to the seas to live the dream again. "Maybe if we were ten years younger," Judith sighs.

Bud is more pragmatic, "We set out to circumnavigate the Caribbean, and we did. You can't just do it again. It wouldn't be the same."

For now they seem content on dry land, adjusting to life on property that used to be part of a cornfield. Judith makes quilts in her spare time, and Bud has a tractor. Their Farmville adventure is just beginning.

⇒ MEETING NEW PEOPLE   41

NEWLY PLANTED
May 2015

I moved to Farmville six years ago, and since that time I've met many wonderful people. The person who has impacted my life perhaps more than any other is Eleanor Kent. I met Eleanor at the Southside Virginia Family YMCA (the Y) where she teaches Yoga, Pilates, and Silver Sneakers. When I first arrived in her classroom, my daily activities were restricted by pain. My physical limitations made me feel less than a complete human. Today, as a direct result of Eleanor's attentive instruction, I am pain free and able to participate fully in my life. I feel like a whole person again.

Not long ago, I had an opportunity to talk with Eleanor and her husband, Will Holliday, about the circumstances that brought them to Farmville.

Eleanor and Will arrived in 2008 when he accepted a position at Longwood University. Will teaches Western Civilization and Latin American History. Additionally, every summer, he takes a group of students to Valencia, Spain, where they explore historically significant places, experience a different culture, and see the tools of democracy at work in an unfamiliar setting.

Will boasts about the accomplishments of his students who accept the challenge of studying abroad. "Every year there are several who have never even flown on a plane before. They learn how to get around the city on their own." He especially enjoys watching young adults grow in confidence as they adjust to foreign customs and learn to communicate with people who speak a different language.

Eleanor also has professional ties to Longwood University. She has worked with students and faculty through various sports teams and clubs, Campus Recreation offerings, and employee health and fitness programs. Her personal connections, however, go even deeper.

"When I was in high school, I attended Girls State," she recalls. And, although she and Will are Virginia Tech alumni, her family includes many former Longwood students. Among them was her grandmother. "I remember her talking about arriving at the train station and having to push her trunk uphill. Now, every time I see the train station, it reminds me of my grandmother."

When Eleanor's grandmother was a student, swimming was required for a degree. "My grandmother hated the water," Eleanor remembers. "She made sure I could swim, so I wouldn't have the struggle she did." The effort paid off. "When I got to teach water aerobics at Longwood, she would have been so proud of me."

Living in Farmville offered Eleanor another surprising opportunity to forge a further connection with her grandmother's memory. "My grandmother always wanted to ride a camel. It was on her bucket list, but she never got to do it. One of my students at the Y told me I could ride a camel at the Amelia County Fair. So in honor of my grandmother, I rode a camel named Clyde and even got to pet him. I didn't have to go to Egypt. I did that right here."

Eleanor and Will enjoy Farmville's small town feel and personal connections. Will likes it when a restaurant's wait staff knows his beverage preference (sweet tea), and he appreciates the camaraderie that develops in a community where work life and social life are intermingled. They both also note that Farmville is centrally located; Richmond, Charlottesville, Lynchburg, and North Carolina are within easy driving distance.

Yet, sometimes their activities take them farther afield. As a fitness instructor, Eleanor takes seriously her commitment to continuing education and keeping her certifications up to date. By participating in classes around the country and in different parts of the world, Eleanor and Will are able to travel and appreciate the diversity of perspectives among the people they meet. But after the adventures, they enjoy coming home.

Recently, Eleanor and Will decided to make a longer-term commitment to the Farmville area and put down roots. Literally. They purchased their first home and bought pansies for their new yard. "I'm discovering the joys of mulching," Will laughs.

Eleanor and Will's story seems to exemplify the essence of Farmville. The past reaches into the present, and then—with some work and cultivation—the future blossoms.

CHECK IT OUT
October 2009

I've had my Farmville Regional Library card longer than I've had my Virginia driver's license. As soon as I rounded up the requisite paperwork proving residency, my first stop was the library. The DMV could wait.

Now, several months later, I can affirm that I'm enjoying my library card more than my driver's license. My driver's license features the state's innovative, high-tech design. If you haven't seen one, let me explain. The picture is black and white. You aren't allowed to smile. In fact, they don't snap the photo until you make the type of face your mother warned you against when she asked, "Do you want your face to freeze like that?"

Theories abound to explain why you can't look happy for your driver's license photo: Some say the authorities require you to wear an expression appropriate for hanging under the word "Wanted." Or, they need to know what you will look like if the police must sift through wreckage to find your remains. My husband prefers the conjecture that the image must be able to endure manipulation by age-progression software. He wants to know if he can preview what the milk cartons will look like should he wander off when he's 106.

My library card doesn't have my picture on it, and it takes me to more places than my driver's license. Behind the wheel, I can visit people and businesses in town and in nearby counties. If I'm feeling especially adventurous, I can check out places like Richmond and Lynchburg. My library card doesn't have such limitations. With it, I can check out virtually any spot on the planet. I can even visit a fair number of other stars and galaxies. I can call on someone in the present, but I can also meet someone from the past. I can glimpse the future. Statesmen and business leaders explain ideals. Scoundrels tell all. Physicists and philosophers. Musicians and mathematicians. They are all in the library.

Even a library on the small side, like the current one in Farmville, is stuffed with more books than I will be able to read during my lifespan. I select library books without premeditation. I can afford to be indiscriminate because they don't cost a thing. I simply walk among the shelves and snatch something that catches my eye or touches my hand. For variety, I might take a book from a top shelf and another from the bottom. If I'm feeling too lazy to bend over or stretch, the middle shelf serves just fine. When I'm really lucky, the librarian points to a title and says, "That's a really good story."

So far, among the titles I have selected, I read the biography of a wise business leader, a collection of short stories about redemption and forgiveness, a courtroom drama highlighting differing standards of justice, and a strange tale of an elderly couple advocating for a special cemetery so that people forced from their homeland during the Second World War could return to be buried.

No matter what the book holds, my goal is to enjoy the experience of reading it. Some books challenge what I believe and make me feel uncomfortable. Some reward me with new understanding. Some are written by masters, and some are poorly done. If I run across an unworthy book, I simply don't finish it. There are too many other wonders waiting to be discovered.

Once the new library building is finished, the expanded shelf space will open up more worlds. And, because it boasts more than a paltry half dozen parking places, I may finally get a chance to enjoy my driver's license.

… CURRENTLY READING

CURLING UP WITH A GOOD BOOK
February 2011

Winter is losing its grip. I've seen a robin, and I've taken a walk without a jacket. But I've been warned that we'll likely have to endure one or two more icy assaults before spring officially arrives. I'm prepared. I've got my easy chair and a stack of books standing by to see me through.

If you're looking for something good to read during the remaining weeks of this winter, here are a few recommendations. But don't rush to the store. These are all available right here, for free, at the Farmville-Prince Edward Community Library.

The Curious Incident of the Dog in the Night-Time, by Mark Haddon. In this book, the narrator is an autistic boy. He describes his efforts to solve the mystery of who killed his neighbor's dog. His comments about how "normal" people function are profound. Furthermore, the window into this particular boy's mind—opening up what he understands of social interaction and what he misunderstands—provides the reader with insights into human relationships. All this is delivered with genuine laughs, poignant moments, and a unique presentation. You can find this one in the adult fiction section.

The Kite Runner, by Kahled Hosseini. This is the story of a young boy who grows up in Afghanistan. The choices he makes and the evil that blooms around him shape the man he becomes. Regrets and personal failures help him understand his own need of redemption and others' need of forgiveness. Although this story is set in unfamiliar circumstances, its themes are universal. This one is also in the adult fiction section.

Cryptonomicon, by Neal Stephenson. In this book, Stephenson presents parallel stories of cryptographers working during World War II and in the present computer age. The parts of the story are offered in intertwined pieces and, like the cryptographers in the story, the reader needs to pay attention to patterns and details in order to work out the intergenerational puzzle. This book isn't science fiction, but perhaps because Stephenson has also written some wonderful science fiction, you'll find this title in the library's science fiction section.

The Art of Racing in the Rain, by Garth Stein. Dogs don't usually write books, but the narrator of this tale is Enzo, the hero's lovable, faithful companion. The author uses the metaphor of racing in the rain—the challenges faced by a race car driver in slippery, hazardous conditions—to look at how people handle the challenges they face in life. The library has only a paperback copy of this book, so you'll need to look for it in the paperback section instead of the regular fiction section.

If you prefer reading about real people, the biography section can be found along the walls on either side of the sitting area in front of the fireplace. One I can recommend is Maya Angelou's, *I Know Why the Caged Bird Sings.* This is the first of Angelou's autobiographical memoirs. In it, she recounts the early years of her life, the challenges of growing up and coming of age amid racial tensions, and her experiences with brutality. Although this sounds grim, the book is really about finding hope.

The library also has a broad collection of non-fiction books. If you haven't been to the library for a while, let me remind you that non-fiction books are arranged by topic using a numerical code called the Dewey Decimal System. For example, if you want to read about philosophy, look in the 100s, religion is in the 200s, and so on. Topics march along until you reach geography and history in the 900s. But, you don't need to memorize the classifications to find a book. With the library's computerized catalog, you can look up any topic you want. If you don't know how to use it, just ask one of the librarians or volunteers to show you.

So if winter still has some surprises in store, you'll find me curled up with a book and a warm blanket. And if you stumble upon a good book during your forays into the library shelves, I hope you'll tell me about it.

READ ANYTHING GOOD LATELY?
February 2012

According to the calendar, we've reached winter's half way point. Although temperatures have been fairly mild, the winter evenings remain long and dark. Perhaps that's why so many people have been asking me if I can recommend any good books.

In fact, I can. I'll begin with the book that has most recently found a spot among my all-time favorites, but because I know not everyone shares my enthusiasm for fantasy and science fiction, I'll also list books in other genres. All these books share one thing in common: You can find each and every one at the Farmville-Prince Edward Community Library.

The Name of the Wind, by Patrick Rothfuss. This book tells the story of Kvothe, whose name means "to know" (and according to the author's website, it is pronounced like the old-fashioned word "quothe"). Throughout the Four Corners of Civilization, Kvothe is a living legend, albeit one with regrets. He narrates the story of his youth, the hardships of being an orphan in an unjust city, and his struggles to gain admittance to a university to learn the physics of magic, the secrets hidden in its library, and the truth about the supernatural beings responsible for the murder of his family. The tale depicts a masterfully crafted world, and the story line extends far beyond a coming-of-age chronicle. It delves into the foundations of prejudice, the misuse of authority, and the true cost of ignorance. The book is the first volume in a trilogy, and you'll find it in the library's Adult Science Fiction section along with the planned trilogy's second volume, *The Wise Man's Fear*. You'll have to wait for the final installment (*The Doors of Stone*). It hasn't yet been published.

The Three Musketeers, by Alexandre Dumas. If you prefer classic literature, you might enjoy this one. Originally written in 1844, this book tells the tale of a young man, d'Artagnan, who travels to Paris to join the musketeers (military guard). The book follows his exploits as he and three other musketeers become embroiled in the schemes of the aristocracy. If you've ever said, "All for one and one for all," you were quoting this book. It's in the library's Adult Fiction section.

Chesapeake, by James A. Michener. Perhaps you want to read a story set a little closer to home. In a style typical of many of his books, Michener combines geological and historical facts to create a fictionalized telling of the way a culture evolves in the face of challenges. This story, spanning four centuries, knits together war, religion, slavery, and politics. It is also in the Adult Fiction section.

The Last Days of Summer, by Steve Kluger. If you're looking for laughs, this one might tickle your funny bone. The story, which takes place in Brooklyn during the early 1940s, involves a boy and his friendship with a baseball star. It is told through pieces of memorabilia, stuff like letters, tickets, postcards, and clippings, which are presented in a scrapbook style. Alas, summer—like innocence—is just for a season. This book is in the library's Young Adult section.

Maybe you'd rather spend the remaining evenings of winter reading to your children or grandchildren. Turn off the television, snuggle up, and let them wrap their imaginations around stories such as *The Wind in the Willows*, by Kenneth Grahame, *Charlotte's Web*, by E.B. White, *Alice in Wonderland*, by Lewis Carroll, *Treasure Island*, by Robert Lewis Stevenson, or any and all of the Harry Potter books by J. K. Rowling. These titles are waiting for you in the library's Children's Area. Although you won't finish reading any of them aloud in a single sitting, you may discover the joy of establishing a family tradition, and in the process your young audience may acquire a life-long love of literature. If you don't have any small people to whom you can read these wonderful stories, perhaps you can enjoy rediscovering them for yourself.

Now, I have a question for you: Have you read any good books lately? If so, I hope you'll share your recommendations with me.

⇒ CURRENTLY READING

FARMVILLE'S LITERARY LANDSCAPE
February 2014

I'm currently reading a novel called *The Third Peril* by L.P. Hoffman. The story opens with a vision George Washington experienced at Valley Forge. An angel appeared and told him the fledgling nation would face three perils. The first was the American Revolutionary War. The second, the U.S. Civil War. And, according to the angel, the third—which arrives in our time—would be the worst of all. Washington asked about its outcome, but didn't receive an answer. I don't know the outcome either because I haven't yet finished the book.

I enjoy Hoffman's story-telling abilities, but there's another wonderful bonus that comes from reading her books—the pleasure of stumbling upon Hoffman herself during my trips into town... at the bookstore, in the library, at a church service. You see, she is a local author.

Farmville and its surrounds are well known for things that grow, such as hay, cows, and chickens. But a different sort of cultivation seems to have sprouted up alongside the fields. The area also hosts a vigorous creative community where inspiration and imagination flourish, and the literary arts are well represented. Writers who live here are working on novels, histories, poems, essays, textbooks, and more. Recently, I've taken an excursion through the literary landscape around Farmville. I'd like to tell you about a few of my discoveries.

Yes Virginia, There Really Is a Farmville, by Marge Swayne, offers an entertaining collection of essays about the trials and tribulations of adjusting to life on a rural farm with some mischievous goats. I learned a lot about the nature of mud and picked up a few pointers regarding what not to do when planting a garden. I also appreciated the reminder to savor the ordinary—and extraordinary—moments that pass by so swiftly every day.

Another book, with a totally different twist on moving to the Farmville area and getting settled in, is *The McGehee Papers*, by W. V. Ligon. This book reprints letters sent by David Burruss McGehee, Jr. to his wife, Sarah Ellen Woodfin, during the middle part of the 1850s. The conversations they share open a window into the private lives of ordinary people who were living during changing times. At the beginning of their marriage, they discuss the challenges of building their home in Cumberland County along the Appomattox River just a few miles from the new railroad.

That new railroad, of course, was the Southside Railroad, which connected Lynchburg with points east and traversed the Appomattox River valley by means of an engineering marvel called High Bridge. *A History of High Bridge*, by Farmville resident J.D. Smith, tells the bridge's story. Smith narrates the original construction, recounts the repairs required during the years after the Civil War, and discusses the modifications required as technologies evolved and trains grew heavier.

Francis Wood, another local author, draws on the past and the present to craft a diverse array of stories. My favorite is *The Teardrop Fiddle*. My fondness for it is likely related to the fact that I have a signed copy I purchased from Wood at Farmville's Heart of Virginia Festival and that very festival plays a role in the story. I also recognize several other landmarks from around town, and that helps me feel directly connected to the action.

Waverly Garner set his debut novel, *Dark Mind*, in the future. In it, Garner considers what would happen if a war between superpowers led to the development of a technology that could turn imagination into a weapon. With the swirling power of a video game, he explores the limits of the human mind and takes his readers on a surrealistic ride through battles and betrayal.

While many of these books can be found at the Farmville-Prince Edward Community Library, the real fun is when you find the authors themselves walking down the street, sipping coffee at your favorite cafe, or standing next to you in line at the grocery store. When this happens, be sure to pass along some encouragement. That kind of support provides the sustenance needed to keep Farmville's literary fields in full bloom.

WINTER READING RECOMMENDATIONS
February 2016

For a few more weeks, cold days will linger and the hours of nighttime darkness will outnumber the hours of sunlight. It's the perfect time of year to settle down with a warm blanket, a cup of hot tea, and a good book. I know just the place to find one.

The Central Virginia Regional Library's two branches serve patrons in the Prince Edward and Buckingham counties and Farmville. I recently asked CVRL staff what books they would recommend.

Nancy Meadows, Library Assistant in Farmville, says, "One book that I've recently enjoyed was *Rogue Lawyer*, by John Grisham. It is currently in the New Fiction section of the library. I enjoyed it because it has colorful characters. It is fast-paced and well written. This book is for adults who enjoy courthouse drama."

Ruth Erdman, Branch Manager in Farmville, recommends *Leviathan Wakes*, by James S. A. Corey. You can find it in Farmville's Science Fiction and Fantasy section. Ruth explains, "If you're a fan of *Star Wars* or *Firefly* then you will love this new series which follows the exploits of James Holden and his crew of ice miners who have been caught up in a conspiracy that could trigger a war between Earth, Mars, and the colonists of the asteroid belt. Catch the new TV series based on the books on SyFy!"

Sonjaye Jackson, Library Assistant in the Buckingham branch also had a suggestion. She recommends *A Summer Affair*, by Susan Wiggs. The book is located in the fiction section at the library. "I recommend this book because it's exciting and takes place in San Francisco. Susan Wiggs captures your attention from the beginning and keeps it until the end of the book. The characters in the story are great and hold wonderful relationships. While reading, everything seems so realistic—as if you are actually one of the characters."

For people who prefer nonfiction, the libraries also offer a wide variety of options. I recently read *Being Mortal: Medicine and What Matters in the End*, by Atul Gawande. The author, who is himself a surgeon, examines the question of how physicians can best offer care to patients who are dealing with the effects of advanced aging or who have terminal diseases. He suggests that medical practitioners should help people not only to have a good life but also to experience death in a manner that allows them to complete their own personal life story in a meaningful way. This book can be found in the Farmville branch. Its call numbers are 362.175 GAW.

I also enjoy reading about astronomy and physics. If you do too, I recommend *A Briefer History of Time*, by Stephen Hawking and Leonard Mlodinow. Don't let the name Hawking scare you off. Although he is one of the foremost physicists of our era, this book is readable and explains a lot about what physicists understand—and don't understand—about the universe in which we live. You'll find this one in the nonfiction section; the call numbers are 523.1 HAW.

The libraries also offer a host of video and electronic resources, including movies on DVD, internet access, subscription database resources for a wide variety of reference materials, and the ability to borrow e-books, digital audio books, and e-magazines. These items can be downloaded directly to your home computer, e-book reader, tablet, or smartphone.

To access these resources—physical and digital—all you need is a library card. If you don't have one, stop by either of the branches and request one. Anyone who lives or works in Buckingham or Prince Edward counties or the town of Farmville or any adjacent county is eligible.

If you haven't recently visited your local library, maybe it's time to find out what you've been missing.

FOR THE BIRDS
February 2010

The yard around our house still stands pretty much naked, an open space where whoever built the house beat the forest back to make room for construction. We have visions of landscaping, or at least planting a few bushes, in the not-too-distant future. Maybe we'll even start a garden. But so far, our biggest yard-related improvement has been the installation of a bird feeder.

We could hear the birds in the trees. Occasionally we'd catch a glimpse as they flitted from one branch to another. We wanted to entice them to venture out to where we could get a better view.

It started as a simple project. We pounded a double shepherd's-crook style hanger into the ground just a few feet from the edge of the woods behind the house so that protective cover would still be close. We unpacked our old birdfeeder, hung it on one of the hooks, and went into town to buy bird food. Several weeks later, we awoke to find pieces of the bird feeder scattered on the ground. Some of them looked chewed.

The woods apparently presented an environment too wild for our dainty suburban feeder. On another trip into town, we fetched a sturdier one. We also bought enough seed to fill a large garbage can, one with a plastic lid that snapped securely in place. We thought this would thwart uninvited critters who might want to plunder the stash. We stored it out back under the deck.

A few weeks later, we needed a new container. Although the sealing mechanism of the lid worked wonderfully well, some mysterious nocturnal guests were not to be hindered. They chewed right through the plastic. Our new garbage can is galvanized, and we keep the lid secured with a bungee cord.

The first guests to make themselves at home at our feeder had tiny ears and bushy tails. No feathers. Squirrels. Even though the feeder was suspended six feet higher than the typical squirrel stands, and even though it was utterly inaccessible via tree branches, and despite their lack of actual flying apparatus, the squirrels had no difficulty reaching the seed. They worked in tandem. One squirrel would scramble up the thin metal pole and fling itself across a perilous gap to land on top of the feeder. Hooking its hind feet at the edge, it would stretch down until it could reach the feeding platform with its forepaws. It then selected the specific seeds it wanted and scattered the rest on the ground below for the other squirrel. They were efficient.

Although watching squirrel antics was amusing, we wondered about how to get birds to come to our feeder if it was either squirrel-draped or barren of seed. A few chickadees made tentative approaches, but the squirrels tenaciously guarded their cache.

Then one rainy afternoon, a squirrel tried to shimmy up the wet metal pole. It attained a height of about two feet and promptly slid back down. I believe a saw a look of astonished incredulity on its face. After it made several attempts, the squirrel gave up. An idea was born. We started spraying non-stick cooking spray on the pole. It doesn't work perfectly. After several days it wears off and needs to be reapplied. The squirrels still make themselves at home, but the tactic keeps them at bay long enough for actual birds to get a turn.

The chickadees began coming regularly. They were followed by wrens, sparrows, and titmice. Then a pair of cardinals and a bluejay and a nuthatch. The winter brought juncos. When we added a suet feeder to the second hook, several woodpeckers delighted us with their visits. And, then one day a flock of wild turkeys wandered through the yard. They didn't seem to actually eat anything we provided. They just waddled by, checking out the ambiance.

So, at long last we've been able to deem the bird feeder project a success. Our feathered friends now seem to feel as welcome as the furry ones.

HUMMING ALONG
July 2010

One day last summer, one of those legendary sultry southern days when the air invites you to soak in it as you might in the sauna at a fancy spa, I was relaxing in the shade of my front porch. My glass of iced coffee was sweating profusely, and I was enjoying the lethargy of the moment—a respite from the normal frantic pace that seems to characterize many of my days.

Without warning, a large insect-like buzz whirred toward my face. I saw its dagger. My scream reflex kicked in. Not exactly a Hollywood-worthy scream, more like an eeping gasp, but still uttered with all the terror I could muster in a nanosecond.

Another nanosecond later, my visual receptors identified the object. It wasn't a giant killer bee aiming for my eyeball. I had experienced a close encounter with a real, live hummingbird. And, I had screamed at it. As quickly as it arrived, it was gone.

I pined for the vanished bird the rest of the summer and resolved that when it returned this year I'd be prepared to make it feel more wanted.

Last autumn, I met Joe Lively, a local author who writes about hummingbirds. Joe's book, *Hummingbirds and the Flowers They Love*, talks about these tiny wonders and provides tips about how to attract them. I studied it from cover to cover. I took notes.

Some other bird guides I consulted also offered information about hummingbirds. I learned that although there is only one kind that frequents this area, the ruby-throated hummingbird, there are hundreds of other varieties in other parts of the world. I learned that their wings beat fifty to sixty times per second and that they are the only kind of bird that can fly backwards. One book described them as "pugnacious." I showed it to my husband, and we laughed recalling my earlier experience.

Armed with my new knowledge, I went to the store to get a hummingbird feeder. I selected a red one with a single artificial flower from which the hummingbird could sip nectar at its leisure. Although Joe's book and several other guides insisted it was a simple matter to make hummingbird nectar, I didn't have enough confidence in my culinary abilities. So, I bought some nectar. When summer arrived, I filled the feeder and waited.

As I watched and wondered how long it would take a hummingbird to discover the feeder, I beheld the amazing answer: About five minutes. But the bird enjoyed no leisurely sip—just a quick slurp. Another hummingbird dive-bombed it and won, for just a moment, a spot at the fount before it, too, was chased off.

I began to fret that the two birds would actually hurt each other, so I returned to the store for a much bigger feeder. It didn't come with dainty, artificial flowers—just a platform with eight feeding holes. I wasn't sure the birds would know what to do. My worry was unnecessary.

At the rate the diminutive visitors gulped nectar, it soon became obvious that the store-bought version was a luxury I couldn't afford for an entire season. I put a kettle on to boil. The birds didn't seem to mind the home brew at all. If anything, they drank with even more abandon.

Although I cannot recognize individuals, I can differentiate the males, with their bright red throats, from the females, who have more subdued green and white markings. I have seen three females vying for a perch and I have seen two males at one time, so I know there are at least five. There may be more.

They share their bounty as well as a group of toddlers. They push each other away, they make scolding clucks, they buzz and dive. They vex. They hassle and tussle. Pugnacious indeed.

And they eat.

I assume that amid all this, somewhere in the trees beyond the yard, the next generation is being prepared to come and join the brawl. At least I hope so, because their whirring buzz is truly one of summer's best delights.

… FEATHERED FRIENDS

THE SOUNDS OF MORNING
May 2013

My favorite way to start the day is with a cup of coffee out on the back porch. I enjoy the quiet prelude before jumping into the demands of the day, but lately I've been noticing just how noisy the quiet can be.

True, I'm not listening to the rush of traffic, the blare of horns, and the squeal of tires (except occasionally when some student is late for class). And, in the solitude of my back yard, I don't hear the mechanical sounds that accompany modern life: the microwave beeping, the refrigerator motor kicking in, or the dryer buzzer announcing that I've got work to do.

But nature, without the hum and whir of appliances, still isn't as quiet as I originally supposed. And the more closely I listen, the more it fills with a symphony of sounds.

Robins seem to enjoy the morning. Their wake up tune goes something like this: "Cheerily, cheer up, cheer up up up." I often feel fairly grumpy in the morning before the caffeine kicks in, but I can't sustain a frown for long under relentless encouragement from the robin community.

Their song competes against a backdrop of other voices. The tufted titmice offer a staccato peep, peep, peep that contrasts with the smoother, lower tones of mourning doves: cooo, oooo, oooo. The chickadees add their two-toned, whee-wha, and a cardinal couple starts proclaiming to each other "birdy, birdy, birdy, birdy." Yes, I smile in agreement, you are indeed birds. The nuthatches think this is pretty funny, too, and they add their own "ha, ha, ha!"

Crows and blue jays work in variations on the same theme. The crows have a deep, caw-caw cackle. The blue jays imitate with a slightly higher, slightly sharper cawk-cawk squawk. When the cowbirds arrive, their voice sounds as if it comes from under water, "Glub, glup."

These songs and calls all meld together into a harmonious whole, and then the true soloists step up to introduce a new melody. A family of Carolina wrens takes its turn, with a lengthy back and forth rendition of chirpety-chirpety-chirpety-chup, cheepa-cheepa-cheepa-chirp.

Then they yield the floor to the goldfinches. I've read accounts of goldfinch songs, and some experts suggest that they are supposed to sound like they're saying "po-ta-to chip." The ones in my backyard apparently find this amusing. They sing, "Really? Real-ly? Hee, hee, hee, hee."

On some mornings, I get a special treat when the exotic jungle-like call of a pileated woodpecker brings things to a crescendo with an eee-eee-eeeech, before the percussion section takes over with a tap, tap, tap, ratta-tatta, ratta-tatta, tap, tap, tap.

And sometimes, there's a sudden rush of wings and a hush. A shadow skims along the edge of my yard, and I know a hawk is circling nearby. Sometimes it enters the area and leaves silently; sometimes it adds its own wheee-ia to the morning's song.

The caesura doesn't last. The wind stirs upper branches. A squirrel rustles though leaves on the ground, and then the song resumes.

When I first started listening to the sounds of the birds in my yard, I couldn't tell them apart. For a long time I mistook a chickadee for a robin. And now that the spring foliage has fully unfurled it is especially challenging to see the individual players. I often find myself questioning: Was that a crow or a blue jay? Who is the mystery songster behind that unfamiliar trill? Who is hiding while singing "pretty bird"? I wish I could see and judge the truth of that statement for myself.

One online resource that has helped identify some of the individuals who sing for me is the Cornel Lab of Ornithology. Their bird guide at http://www.allaboutbirds.org includes facts, videos, and recorded songs. I've also been learning a lot from the Virginia Master Naturalist program, and I'm looking forward to a bird field trip later this spring.

Eventually, after listening to the songs and calls, I notice that either my coffee is gone or gone cold. I know it is time to head inside and begin my day, but now the indoor racket seems quiet and empty.

I'M A BIRDWATCHER
June 2014

A birdwatcher is someone who sits in a comfortable chair on a porch or by a window and watches birds that happen to flap or wander by. If the local feathered friends are shy, a birdwatcher will hang a feeder to lure them into view. A birdwatcher probably has a mug of coffee or glass of iced tea at hand. On warm days, birdwatchers sometimes partake in unscheduled catnaps.

Real avian enthusiasts prefer the term birder. Birders get up before the crack of dawn. They don't wait for birds to come to them. They creep through the underbrush and sneak peeks into natural habitats. Birders don't seem to worry about ticks or getting tangled in spider webs. They recognize birdsong—not because they listened to a recording but because they've watched performances of it being sung. Birders carry binoculars, and they never fall asleep on the job.

Farmville's Margaret H. Watson Bird Club (http://www.farmville birders.net) offers a friendly mix of birders and birdwatchers. I've learned a lot from their programs, and I've never felt maligned because of my aversion to early morning tromps through the thorny verge. During the club's past year of programs, I had a chance to meet some native owls (and to enjoy owl-shaped cookies) and view a presentation about bluebirds. I'm lucky to have the kind of habitat bluebirds require right behind my house. Although they don't come to my seed or suet feeders, they sit on the telephone wire and keep an eye on everyone else, including cardinals, goldfinches, nuthatches, indigo buntings, and woodpeckers of several varieties.

While watching the birds at my feeders this spring, I had a surprise. From an upstairs window, I noticed an unusual bird at the suet feeder. It was on a corner perch typically frequented by a downy woodpecker, but it was bigger. Also, the black and white of its back formed a different pattern with much more contrast. Hobnobbing with birders apparently had produced some effect. I ran for my binoculars.

The new bird was certainly no woodpecker. It was something altogether new. It had a large, but rather stubby, bill. When it turned to face me, I saw a red triangular patch on its breast—not red like the rust of a robin, but the brilliant red of a bright cardinal. As I watched in awe, another amazing thing happened. A second novel bird walked around from the back of the feeder. The latest new arrival was about the same size but looked entirely different. It wore a streaked brownish-grey plumage and had a white stripe over its eye. Two new birds at one time! I was puzzled by how well they got along together. My woodpeckers usually don't share. They have to wait turns.

To unlock the mystery of the recent arrivals, I went scurrying for my bird books. Flipping through the photographs, I saw it: rose-breasted grosbeak. The male had the black, white, and red markings. The female was brown with a generous stroke of white eyeliner. Seeing them together left me with no doubt about who was visiting my feeder.

I was eager to tell someone. Fortunately, a day later I ran into Evan Spears, a member of the Margaret H. Watson Bird Club. He let me gush about my wonderful new birds, and when I paused to catch my breath, he agreed that they were spectacularly beautiful birds. "Enjoy them," he encouraged. But then he added, "They're just passing through during their migration. They won't stay."

No, no! I wanted to say. They loved my backyard. I wanted them to stick around all summer. But of course, they didn't. True to their nature, and in accordance with Evan's prediction, they were soon gone.

The thrill of seeing something new, something unusual, gave me a better understanding about why someone would be willing to get out of bed so early on a Saturday morning to go tromping through mud and brambles. I confess that I'm not yet ready for the full adventure, but I am looking forward to fall when the bird club will resume its programming schedule.

ROOTING FOR THE RAVENS
April 2016

Let me begin with a note to sports fans: The ravens I'm rooting for don't wear football helmets.

Ravens of the feathered kind have haunted my imagination for as long as I can remember. There's the fable attributed to Aesop in which a raven learns, albeit too late, about the perils of harming others. Ravens play supporting roles in several fairytales, and my penchant for Arthurian legend and related literature introduced me to multiple raven characters drawn from references sprinkled throughout Celtic mythology. One Native American story tells of the raven who brought fire from the sun to the earth, and another tale attributes creation itself to a raven. And, of course, there's the famous Nevermore from Edgar Allan Poe's poem, The Raven.

Storybook and mythical ravens such as these often play ambiguous roles associated with the boundary between life and death. They carry messages between the spiritual world and the physical one. They are linked with prophecy and wisdom; they are linked with doom and destiny. Poe exploited this duality in his poem. At first, the narrator welcomes the bird, who promises steadfast companionship, never to leave "as hopes have flown before." Later, when macabre imagination envisions the raven as a sinister visitor from beyond the grave, the narrator fears it and rails against it. Yet at the poem's end, the raven "still is sitting, still is sitting" above the door. Having spent my own requisite number of midnights dreary, pondering, weak and weary, I've come to believe that Poe's abiding raven signifies the way life's events can shape us. Sometimes for good, and sometimes not, but always for evermore.

Because of their multifaceted literary symbolism and their persistence across so many different cultures and millennia, I developed a fondness for ravens. Or, at least a fondness for the idea of them. I'd never actually met a raven. Until last year.

Happy to Be Here

Last spring, a pair of nesting ravens took up residence in one of the steel towers at High Bridge. Apparently, in more natural environments, some ravens build nests under an overhang on a cliff face. The bridge's substructure provides an analogous, man-made setting: a high platform under a protective roof. The birds were promptly named Raymond and Ramona. Bob Flippen, Education Specialist at High Bridge Trail State Park, now also known as the Raven Whisperer, provided updates on the growing family. As often as I could, I stopped by their nest to peer in.

Although I hate to admit it, the hatchlings were sort of ugly. Their nearly naked, lumpy bodies didn't even look bird-like. To their doting parents, however, they must have been wonderful. Eventually, the babies sprouted black feathers. For a while they seemed to be about half beak and half bird. The beaks were always open, and the parents kept bringing dinner. By the time the fledglings were ready to fly, their bodies had grown large enough to make their mouths appear more suitably proportional. It reminded me of the way a puppy sometimes needs to grow into its feet.

The young fliers soon became as sleek and aerobatically proficient as their parents. They swooped and soared above and below the bridge and among the trees that line the Appomattox Valley. Sometimes they would stand on the bridge's railing, their deep, black eyes watching, always watching. I felt as if they were studying me. Sometimes it seemed that the ravens had something profound to say, if only I were equipped to listen. Then, at the end of summer, they flew away.

The Cornell Lab of Ornithology's All About Birds website claims, "Ravens are among the smartest of all birds, gaining a reputation for solving ever more complicated problems." They used to be more common in our area, but the population declined as a result of habitat loss during the 19th and early 20th centuries. In recent decades, however, ravens have been making a comeback.

Last month, Bob Flippen reported that Raymond and Ramona had returned to their nest. New hatchlings made their appearance on March 13th. I'm looking forward to another season of watching them take flight. Perhaps this year, if I'm worthy, I'll hear their message.

Four-Legged Fauna

WHY DID THE TURTLE CROSS THE ROAD?
May 2011

One of my favorite "gadgets" (a small computer program) creates turtles on my monitor. They swim at the edge of a digital pond and crawl on a simulated shore. When I feed them with a click of my computer's mouse, they respond enthusiastically with scrabbling feet and bobbling heads. I am amazed at how comforting it is to watch them.

I shouldn't be surprised. My heros have always been turtles.

First, there was Mack, the turtle at the bottom of the stack in Dr. Seuss's *Yertle the Turtle*. If it's been a while since you have encountered children's books, I'll remind you that King Yertle was ruler over all he could see. He ordered his subject turtles to stand one atop the other, making a high tower, and then a higher one, so he could see farther and farther. Mack complained, to no avail, about his knees and his back. In the end, with a simple burp, Mack toppled the tower. Yertle tumbled, and once humbled, he ended up being ruler of only the mud.

Later, when my reading level rose, I encountered the turtle at the beginning of John Steinbeck's *The Grapes of Wrath*. Steinbeck spends an entire chapter explaining how one turtle laboriously works to cross the highway. Its journey is perilous. A sedan swerves to avoid it. A truck swerves to hit it. Steinbeck writes that the "front wheel struck the edge of the shell, flipped the turtle like a tiddly-wink, spun it like a coin, and rolled it off the highway."

I've often felt like that poor turtle. Sometimes it seems like the events of life whizz by, flipping me this way and that, leaving me struggling in the dust trying to regain my footing. Steinbeck's heroic fellow pulls into its shell for a while, but then the feet come out. It rights itself and continues on its way. A role model for perseverance in the face of adversity.

This time of year, it becomes increasingly common to see turtles in the road. They leave ponds where they have hibernated during the winter and seek good places to lay their eggs.

One of the things that appeals to me about Farmville is the willingness many folk have to honor these creatures by helping them cross the road. Many times, I have pulled up behind a car that stopped so a turtle could safely pass. Sometimes a driver or passenger will even get out of the car to carry the turtle on its way to the other side of the road. My husband and I have even had the privilege of participating in the ritual. In fact, our route into town seems to include a spot that is especially favored by turtles for crossing. For a while last spring, we stopped so frequently that my husband wouldn't ask if I was ready to leave for an errand. Instead he'd say, "Are you ready to go rescue a turtle?"

Not all turtles are lucky, however, and I have been saddened to sometimes encounter the crushed remains of one that didn't make it across the road. I'd like to believe the unfortunate event was unavoidable rather than the result of intentional malice. Turtles don't dash out in front of cars the way squirrels do. But they don't scamper out of the way either. I suppose occasionally they aren't seen in time. Or perhaps tailgating traffic makes slowing or stopping too hazardous to attempt.

But on the whole, Farmville is a place where life—even the slow-moving kind—is respected. And Good Samaritans not only move lumbering waddlers out of harm's way, they take the time for people, too. They hold doors open rather than let them slam shut on others behind them. They send notes of encouragement. They let people go ahead of them in line at the grocery store. They give to those in need and lend an ear or a hand just for the asking.

So now not all my heros are turtles. Some of them are people.

//= FOUR-LEGGED FAUNA 65

MOOOOVING ALONG
October 2012

You may have noticed my affection for cows. The doodle that accompanies this column even features a friendly cow sitting on a porch swing.

Cow pastures line the roads around Farmville. When you drive into or out of town you usually do so under the watchful eye of some cow. They lend a tranquil ambience to the countryside, creating scenery that is pastoral and peaceful. There are rolling hills, hay fields, picturesque fences, occasional streams, stands of majestic trees, and herds of noble cows.

Cows are also fun. The cows that live in the pasture at the end of my street certainly seem easygoing and good natured. When I'm sitting outside and I hear a distant moo-oo, I think I have a four-legged friend telling me the joke of the day. It always makes me smile.

The farmers among us have undoubtedly noticed that my ideas about cows lack touches from the department of reality. The plain truth of the matter is that I had never met a real cow in person. Until last month.

My husband and I were biking along High Bridge Trail when we rounded a curve and came upon a cow. It straddled the path. We skidded to an abrupt halt, and I immediately learned three new things about cows:

The closer they are the bigger they are. Cows on a distant hillside are visually about the size of play things, and calfs seem as cuddly as kittens. Up close, cows are larger than elephants. At least I'm sure this one was. And it looked about as cuddly as a well-muscled, heavily armed gangster.

Soft cow eyes are for the comics. Recall any artful cow image you've seen. Remember those big, kindhearted eyes? Fantasy. Real cow eyes are wary. The one blocking our path glowered at us. The phrase "If looks could kill..." came to mind. We backed away slowly.

Real cows aren't placid. The cow standing in front of us didn't moo a greeting at all. It snorted at our puny presence. Its tail swished and snapped like the smack of a fly swatter. There was no doubt in my mind which of us was being invited to play the role of the fly.

So there we stood. And the cow wasn't giving an inch.

I did some mental math. From where we were standing, if there wasn't a cow in the path, it was six miles to where we left the car. If we turned around to make our way back by going all the way around the world, it would be about 25,000 miles, minus six, for a total of 24,994 miles. Then, if I could ride at about ten miles an hour and keep it up for ten hours a day, I figured I'd get back to the car in eight or nine months. For a moment, that seemed more feasible than getting past the cow. Then I remembered about the oceans.

My husband, the brave and practical member of our family, was more concerned that the cow would continue its sojourn and wander out onto the highway. That could make for a very bad day for the cow, not to mention any cars it happened to encounter. In a smooth quick draw, he whipped out his cell phone.

Shortly thereafter we were rescued by High Bridge Trail State Park's chief ranger, Craig Guthrie. He told us, "Cows are really smart animals. She probably knows exactly where she's supposed to be."

The cow nodded in agreement, but apparently where she was supposed to be was on the other side of where we were. She dipped her head again and charged forward. I must have closed my eyes because I didn't see her veer. She went by without any mayhem and continued trotting on her way. Officer Guthrie later told us that she went straight to a nearby farm and selected a specific gate. He opened it for her, and the story had a happy ending.

And, yes, I still love cows. But now I know that an essential ingredient of any idyllic pastoral scene is a sturdy fence.

ON THE NATURE OF MICE
June 2013

I used to think mice were cute. My mental image focused on their furry little bodies, oversized ears, and earnest eyes. Small and fluffy. Tiny pink toes and little pink noses.

The roots of this misperception can be traced to my growing up years. Mickey Mouse was a bashful hero and Minnie was his gal. Then Mighty Mouse came to save the day. He was a more muscular rodent, able to vanquish the powers of evil and defend the American way.

Cartoons weren't the only basis of my knowledge about mousedom. I also learned a lot about the nature of mice from other sources. For example, in Hans Christian Anderson's *Thumbelina*, a mouse rescues the eponymous heroine from starving. They strike a deal, and she agrees to tell him stories and clean his house in exchange for food and shelter during the harsh winter months. The plan sours when the mouse tries to arrange a marriage between the thumb-sized maiden and his neighbor, the mole, but I always believed the mouse's intentions were honorable.

Other literary mice communicated additional messages about rodent virtue. Stuart, the diminutive surprise born to Mr. and Mrs. Little in E. B. White's classic tale, was always polite and helpful. He demonstrated how to navigate in a world fraught with perils and inhabited by much bigger folk. In Aesop's fable "The Lion and the Mouse," I learned about the rewards of being merciful. *The Chronicles of Narnia*, by C. S. Lewis, included the courteous but fearless mouse Reepicheep, who taught me that you can be brave and praiseworthy even if you're small.

I also had connections to mice outside their presence in literature. One of my first artistic accomplishments was learning to make fingerprint mice. I'd use pencil or ink on my index finger and press it against some paper. Next, I added ears, eyes, nose, a smile, and whiskers. Then, with a flourish, I'd draw a curling tail. Voila! A mouse.

When I learned to embroider, I made samplers in which mice played starring roles. When I became a mother, I tucked my children into their beds with fluffed pillows and stuffed mice. I read *If You Give a Mouse a Cookie* over and over and over. Cute.

I know I'm not the only person who was duped into thinking mice were cute. If you want evidence, just peruse the greeting card section of your favorite store. You'll see adorable mice depicted as kindly, industrious, and cuddly. They outsmart cats, deliver punch lines, and proffer flowers. They even share their cheese.

My delusion started to unravel one day when my husband and I got into his car. An old handkerchief lay across the passenger's seat. "What's this doing here?" I asked. He said he didn't know. It was supposed to be in the center console where he kept it in case something needed to be wiped off.

I picked up the handkerchief. It was full of holes. "Maybe you need a new one," I suggested. Then, I opened the glove box. It was a nest of shredded papers, apparently the remains of our car manual. "Um..." I said and pointed.

"A mouse!" he concluded. That night he set a trap. The next morning, our peanut butter offering had been gingerly licked away from the non-springing parts. Secretly, I was glad the mouse got away because part of me still embraced the notion that mice were cute.

Then, about a week later, the "Check Engine" light came on. So, we got the engine checked. It turns out that one of the hoses necessary for properly venting combustion by-products had a hole chewed in it. "Looks like a mouse," the repair technician said. "That'll be $400." And he regaled us with stories about other mouse-chewed cars where repairs ran into the thousands.

Cute? Well, perhaps. But, now that my mouse education has been expanded to include a few realities from rural life, Laura Numeroff's children's tale seems more erudite than I previously understood: If you give a mouse a cookie, or even an old handkerchief, the cycle of what the mouse wants next never ends.

… FOUR-LEGGED FAUNA

BAFFLED
October 2013

My husband used to have a T-shirt with an image on it that caused people to look twice. On a first hasty glance, it appeared to be a blue jay carrying a sign that said, "Feed the birds!" But something about the bird seemed a little odd, and that's what led to the second looks. It was really a squirrel in a bird costume. It had a beak strapped around its face, wings fastened to its forearms, and feathers hiding a bushy tail. It was all dressed up for trick or treating. And, when it comes to squirrels, I have to admit most of the tricks have been on us.

We've been engaged in a contest of wits with our backyard squirrel population ever since we hung our first birdfeeder. Our yard ends at a tree line that includes several varieties of oak. Squirrels are supposed to like acorns, so we weren't surprised to see them scurrying around among the branches. What has been amazing is their tenacity and creativity in raiding the birdseed.

I suppose we were naive to think squirrels would be thwarted by the six-foot pole we used to mount our feeder. As it turns out, pole climbing is a skill mastered in squirrel kindergarten. They would scamper up the pole and drape themselves across the feeder. The first squirrels to reach the summit would pick out the choicest seeds and fling the rest to the ground so all their kin could eat. The process would continue at a frenetic pace until the seeds were gone.

We got the first laugh when we put non-stick cooking spray on the pole. Squirrels would start up the pole and slide back down. We chortled. They were indignant. Then they got even. They learned how to grip the pole and climb up anyway.

Our next strategy was a squirrel baffle. It's a conical device that attaches to the pole below the feeder in a way that squirrels (theoretically) can't get past. In addition to being a confounding obstacle, the baffle presents an unstable surface. When a squirrel grabs its edge, the cone wobbles and the squirrel falls. Our squirrels were flummoxed for several days before they figured out how reach past it by holding the rim firmly against the pole with their hind feet.

It took us several months to figure out that a series of differently sized baffles could be spaced so that the squirrels couldn't traverse the gaps. We thought we'd won, but the squirrels just moved to a new battleground. They learned how to take the metal lid off the galvanized aluminum can we keep under the back porch for storing the birdseed. We got a sturdy chain, clamped the lid down, and felt smug.

That victory celebration was cut short when once again a squirrel appeared atop the birdfeeder. The mystery of how a squirrel was managing to reclaim its position atop the birdfeeder lasted for weeks. We never saw one climb the pole. We checked the closest trees, and none of their branches were even remotely within reach. And yet, apparently out of thin air, a squirrel appeared atop the bird feeder with some regularity.

One day, I was standing by the window and a blurred movement caught my eye. It seemed to be something falling out of the sky. I looked to the ground. A squirrel. I thought it must have fallen out of a tree. I looked up trying to estimate the distance. The squirrel got up and walked off. It seemed a bit stunned. I watched it climb a tree and repeat the stunt. This time it landed squarely on top of the birdfeeder. I didn't believe my eyes. It was jumping across a span of more than 10 feet.

I don't think my husband believed my story until several days later when he witnessed a repeat performance. He retaliated by cutting the offending branch from the tree. With that platform removed, it was several days before we once again found a squirrel atop the birdfeeder. I still don't know how it got there. I'm baffled.

LYING DOWN ON THE JOB
March 2015

I had always heard that cows lie down before earthquakes. So, when I noticed the frequency with which cows around Farmville reclined in their fields, it was rather alarming. Based on my casual observations, on any given day, it seemed nearly half our local bovine population expected tremblers. I'm delighted to report that their earthquake prediction accuracy, at least thus far, has been fairly dismal.

It would make sense for cows to lie down before earthquakes. After all, there is that story about a cow being swallowed up during the infamous San Francisco earthquake of 1906. The tale goes like this: The quake opened a fissure. A cow (Matilda in some versions of the story, nameless in others) belonging to a Mr. Shafter fell in. The earth suddenly snapped back together leaving only the animal's tail visible. Or the tail and head. Or the feet. The U.S. Geological Survey thinks the story was fabricated and told to a gullible newspaper reporter.

Nevertheless, the suspected ability of cows to predict earthquakes was studied in 2008 by a team of researchers from the Swedish University of Agricultural Sciences. According to a news story in *The Local*, a British newspaper that reports on Swedish news, scientists fitted eight cows with GPS sensors and monitors. When an earthquake struck southern Sweden on December 16, 2008 its epicenter was only five kilometers from the cows. Researchers reported results for seven of the cows (monitoring equipment on the eighth failed): Two cows standing before the event remained standing, and two cows lying down remained lying down. Three cows changed their positions. Two that had been lying down stood up, one shortly before the quake began and the other as it began. At the same time, one that had been standing chose that moment to lie down. A spokesperson for the research team claimed that, despite the small sample size, it was reasonable to conclude that cows did not have any special sensory awareness of impending earthquakes.

I'd also heard a theory that cows lie down when it's going to rain. According to that notion, cows can sense changes in the air. When barometric pressure goes up, they lie down to ease their stomachs. Or, when the humidity goes up in advance of a shower, a cow lies down to keep a spot of grass dry. Apparently, neither of these suppositions is true, and it also isn't true that cows lie down to cool off in the grass when the weather is hot. According to *Modern Farmer*, a study done by Dr. Jamison Allen (formerly of the University of Arizona) found exactly the opposite. Cows stand up when they're hot. Standing increases their body surface area and causes heat to dissipate more efficiently.

After reaching these dead ends in my quest to understand why so many cows seemed to be lying down on the job, I decided I needed to do my own investigation. I asked someone with experience, Farmville resident Jo Smith. Her family raises cows (among other things), so I figured she'd know.

For starters, Jo told me cows stand when they graze, but they don't chew the grass while grazing. They munch quickly and store the grass in a special stomach. Then they lie down, get comfortable, and regurgitate (more correctly, ruminate) the grass for leisurely chewing. The process is called "chewing their cud." I'd heard the phrase before. Everyone knows cows chew their cud, but I never really understood what it meant. It seems similar to the human tendency to sit down to enjoy a meal after standing to prepare it.

Jo also told me cows lie down to go to sleep. A horse can sleep standing up, but a cow can't lock its knees the way a horse does. It has to lie down. Furthermore, each individual cow simply decides if and when it wants to stand up or lie down. Sometimes, they just don't feel like standing.

Jo's cows aren't dairy animals, so I didn't ask her: What do you get if you milk a cow during an earthquake? Anyway, that's one answer I do know: Milkshakes.

FLUTTER BY
April 2012

I had been waiting for the butterflies.

When we lived in Michigan, I always waited for the robins, well known as harbingers of spring. Some years, they'd show up in early March but in others they wouldn't make an appearance until April. Eagerly looking for them to return from their southern sojourn added a touch of excitement to the annual ritual of bidding winter adieu. Perhaps partly in honor of the bird's role in delivering hope to winter-weary folk, Michigan named the robin its state bird in 1931. Here in Farmville, however, robins make poor heralds of spring. Apparently, this is where some of them spend the winter.

So I was in the market for more geographically appropriate signs of spring. A neighbor suggested butterflies.

No one knows how butterflies came to be called butterflies. Various speculations exist—they are flies that like butter, or a type of insect that excretes a butter-like substance, or possibly some are the color of cream or butter. *The Oxford English Dictionary*, a recognized authority on the histories of words, claims that the real reason remains unknown. My father, who liked to make up his own words, was fond of transposing the consonant sounds. He called them "flutterbies." And that is what butterflies do best. They flutter by.

Butterflies seem particularly well-suited to the role of spring portents. They begin their lives as tiny eggs, usually attached to the underside of leaves. Each species has its own preferred plant hosts. When baby caterpillars emerge from these eggs, they are eating machines.

They eat and they grow, and then the magic begins. Once a caterpillar reaches its full size, it moves into a life state called the pupa, and it encases itself in a chrysalis (commonly called a cocoon, but technically cocoons are structures made by moths). They appear to hang lifeless. But far from being dead, they undergo a process called metamorphosis from which they emerge as something altogether different. The butterfly unfurls its wings and takes to the air.

As spring rolls around, that's exactly what the year does. New years are birthed on the underside of the shortest, darkest days of winter. They seem to hang around for a bit in a state of dormant anticipation, and then they are transformed. Somehow without noticing the passage of time, three months are spent. Days begin to flit by, nigh uncatchable.

According to the website http://www.thebutterflysite.com, the state of Virginia is home to 69 different kinds of butterflies, ranging in size from as small as my thumbnail to as big as my hand. With so many, I was surprised to discover that the state officially honors one specific butterfly. I knew there was a state bird (cardinal) and a state flower and tree (dogwood), but I didn't know that the Eastern Tiger Swallowtail Butterfly (scientific name *Papilio glaucus*) was the state's official insect. The designation was sanctioned under a 1991 revision of subsection 1-510 of the Code of Virginia, relating to official emblems and designations. Several other states also recognize this fairly common butterfly: Delaware, Georgia, South Carolina, and Alabama. In fact, Alabama honors two butterflies, the Eastern Tiger Swallowtail (as official butterfly) and the Monarch butterfly (as official insect).

This year, I saw my first butterfly several weeks ahead of the calendar's designation of spring. It seemed a tiny, lonely thing as it hovered near the edge of a fallen tree, but my heart connected with it, and I felt the year undergo its metamorphosis. As the subsequent days passed, trees budded and bloomed. Flowers stretched up from the ground and shook the dirt off their petals. Goldfinches turned bright yellow, and the year's first crop of baby squirrels peeked out on to a new world.

As I get older, every year seems to flit by faster than the one before. I'm sure this one will be no exception. But, I hope I get a chance to chase at least a few of the days. Perhaps I'll even catch one or two so that I can enjoy their beauty before they all flutter by.

BELOVED BEES
March 2016

I've been reading information from the Xerces Society, an organization formed to promote the conservation of insects and other invertebrates. They claim that bumblebees are the "best-loved" of all the bees.

Bees, bumble and otherwise, certainly have my respect. As tireless, industrious workers, bees pollinate many different kinds of plants, thereby ensuring that fruits and seeds continue to develop. They play a vital role in the chain of events that keeps flowers in my garden and food on my table. But I'd never actually considered loving a bee. The stinger presents a sufficient threat to keep my admiration from blossoming into passion.

Perhaps bumblebees are best-loved in the sense that they are the least feared. Their roly-poly roundness does suggest a child-like playfulness, and the dense hairs that cover their bodies vaguely resemble fur. One of my children once had a stuffed animal creature that combined teddy bear characteristics with bumblebee coloration, wings, and antennae. That hybrid beast certainly had the stuffing loved out of it.

Bumblebees also hold the distinction of being among the first bees to emerge in the spring. Mated queens hibernate through the cold months, and they emerge with the earliest flowers to start the tasks of building nests and collecting nectar to feed the next generation. Because they serve as harbingers of warmer weather, I'm usually happy to see them appear.

When I first moved to the Farmville area, I mistook another type of bee for a kind of bumblebee. It looked similar, but had a shiny abdomen rather than a furry one. A neighbor corrected me and explained that what I saw was a carpenter bee.

The word carpenter led me to envision a skilled tradesman who could take a pile of wood and turn it into something useful, like cabinets and furniture. Carpenters wield an impressive array of dangerous-looking tools, and they can hit a nail with such precision that their fingers remain unscathed. A carpenter built my house and my back deck.

The concept of a carpenter bee intrigued me. I wondered what these magnificent insects might construct. Did they make rocking chairs for queen bees to use when singing lullabies to their brood? Did honey bees hire them to make honeycombs? Did bumblebees ask them to build storage sheds for pollen reserves? Perhaps the one hanging around my house simply wanted to pick up a few tips from the professionals who constructed it. Imagine my disappointment when I learned that carpenter bees didn't seek to admire the workmanship involved in building homes and decks. They just wanted to chew through them. It seems that the only thing carpenter bees have in common with carpenter humans is their tendency to create sawdust.

On the other hand, carpenter bees do work diligently alongside bumblebees to pollinate my garden's tomatoes, and I am quite fond of home-grown tomatoes.

Still, it was necessary to defend my house. I had a conversation with the carpenter bee that seemed to have claimed my back deck as its personal territory. I explained that a vast number of trees, natural wood sources it could use to its heart's delight, lay just beyond my yard. The bee buzzed and wagged. I think it was trying to explain that what I thought of as a back deck was actually just a stack of wood laid out in an attractive buffet. Furthermore, he seemed convinced that his claim on it took precedence over mine. Clearly, we were at an impasse.

A bit of research revealed that carpenter bees prefer their wood unpainted. My husband organized our counterattack, and this year we're ready to stand our ground with freshly painted deck railings.

Bees—carpenter, bumble, and otherwise—play such a vital role in sustaining a healthy ecosystem I'm ready to offer them a certain amount of grudging affection. Full blown ardor and the exchanging of hugs and kisses will have to wait until they agree to do something about their stinger problem. Until then, I'll love watching from a distance as they work to pollinate my plants.

TWINKLE, TWINKLE, LITTLE BUG
June 2016

Light fascinates me. It comes in so many different forms. Fireworks, sparklers, Christmas displays. Flames that lap the air from a campfire. The red-hot glow of coals in a barbecue. I love sunshine, the warmth of it and the dappled patterns it makes on the ground when filtered through a tree in full leaf. I love the glitter path created by a moonrise over a lake. I'm enchanted by the stars.

And when summer arrives, the magic of little insects flashing in the darkness leaves me spellbound. I feel an affinity with every child who has ever dreamed of seeing a fairy. Lightning bugs—or fireflies—offer a tantalizing hope that an enchanted realm lurks within the woods. The child in me still wants to chase the flash and capture a dream.

But what exactly are they?

Some people say lightning bug. Some say firefly. Both terms refer to the same type of insect. According to linguistic research, the term firefly is more common in the western parts of the United States. Lightning bug is more commonly used in parts of the Midwest. The terms are used interchangeably in many eastern regions. But, whether you call them fireflies or lightning bugs, technically they are neither flies nor true bugs.

Flies belong to the Diptera order of insects. Flies have two full wings instead of four like other groups of insects. House flies, deer flies, and crane flies are all flies. So are midges, no-see-ums, and even mosquitos. In fact, there are approximately 160,000 different kinds of flies around the world, and 20,000 in the U.S. and Canada. But fireflies are not among them.

The word bug is often used casually to refer to any small insect, but from an entomological perspective, true bugs are insects that belong to the order Hemiptera, a term that refers to the partially hardened portion of their forewings. True bugs include cicadas, aphids, and stink bugs. Globally, there are approximately 82,000 different species of true bugs, with about 12,000 in North America. True bugs have a mouth designed to suck nutrients from a food source. Some of them are true pests, associated with crop damage and the spread of diseases. Others are benign or even beneficial. But lightning bugs are not bugs in this sense.

Lightning bugs belong to the order Coleoptera, that is, beetles. Coleoptera is the largest single order in the entire animal kingdom, comprised of 350,000 species; 25,000 in North America. Beetles have hard bodies, their mouths are designed for chewing, and they possess two pairs of wings, although the forewings are used primarily as a cover for the flying wings. The thing that makes lightning bugs—or fireflies—special is a characteristic known as bioluminescence. The underside of a firefly's abdomen contains an organ that combines chemicals to produce light. According to National Geographic, there are 2,000 different firefly species.

Each type of firefly has its own unique timing and pattern of flashing. The Common Eastern Firefly (*Photinus pyralis*) lights up while flying in a J-pattern. Another type, known by the scientific name *Photinus brimleyi*, presents a single yellowish flash about every ten seconds. The Woods Firefly (*Photuris pennsylvanica*) displays double flashes of greenish light that repeat every two or three seconds. *Photinus macdermotti* presents a yellowish double flash in a sequence that repeats every four to five seconds. The Blue Ghost Firefly (*Phausis reticulata*) glows in a steady, pale blue-green light for about 30 seconds.

One of the most spectacular displays comes from the Synchronous Firefly (*Photinus carolinus*). This species displays five to eight flashes of light in a pattern that repeats every eight to ten seconds. As the name implies, groups of these insects flash in a synchronized pattern, and depending on how they are spread across an area, the flashes may occur in waves.

Most of these species are fairly common, and in the U.S. you can observe them in early summer throughout many parts of the East and Midwest. Synchronous fireflies are less common. They live only in a small region near the southern Appalachians. Great Smoky Mountains National Park, which spans portions of North Carolina and Tennessee, is famous for its annual displays. Here in Farmville, High Bridge Trail State Park hosts its annual Firefly Festival in June. The event offers park visitors an opportunity to experience the magic as thousands of fireflies twinkle and blink in the trees below their feet.

Caring for the Yard and the World

SNAKE IN THE GRASS
September 2010

Since the moment we decided to move to Virginia, my husband has been fascinated by snakes. Michigan, where we used to live, is home to a mere 17 different varieties of snake (compared with 30 species in Virginia), and only one, the massasauga rattlesnake, is venomous.

We encountered a massasauga once during a walk in a park in southeast Michigan. While strolling through a meadow toward a small lake, I took a step in some tall grass and heard the rattle. There was no mistaking it. I froze, and then I saw it. Coiled and ready to strike. Next to my foot. I jumped, and my husband helped propel me as far from it as possible. We backed away slowly, and eventually the snake did the same. My husband says it was about 28 inches long, but my memory suggests it was closer to six or eight feet. Well, three at least.

Such a snake encounter in Michigan is a rare event. The massasauga rattlesnake is even protected by state law because their numbers have been so reduced as a result of habitat loss and what the state's Department of Natural Resources calls "persecution by humans."

Here in Virginia, snakes seem to be more abundant, and several varieties are venomous: cottonmouths (water moccasins), copperheads, timber rattlesnakes, and canebrake rattlesnakes. The canebrake rattlesnake, an endangered inhabitant of the Dismal Swamp, doesn't seem to pose a significant danger, but the copperhead appears to be ubiquitous.

To be prepared for this new threat, my husband set out to learn how to identify and avoid copperheads. The Virginia Herpetological

Society website (http://www.virginiaherpetologicalsociety.com) offers snake-related information, including an extensive review comparing copperheads to harmless snakes. He studied the pictures. He took the online "copperhead test." He quizzed me until I could recite the facts, too: Copperheads have markings that are shaped like an hour glass, wide on the snake's sides with the narrow portion near its top. Once, while walking on High Bridge Trail State Park, we spotted a copperhead sunning itself. We gave it a wide berth, and it ignored us. Our snake defense strategy seemed to be working.

Then one evening, my husband asked if there was anything in particular I wanted to do. A quick glance at the calendar revealed nothing. "No," I said, and I think I added, "If you want some excitement, you'll have to come up with something yourself." He thought the rare, free evening would be perfect for catching up on some yard work, and I went on my merry way puttering around the house. I talked to my daughter on the phone. I checked my e-mail.

Then the back door opened, and my husband hollered for me to come quickly. I heard the urgency in his voice and ran. "I've just been bitten by a copperhead," he said, but not quite that calmly. There may have been an expletive added.

All our reading suggested that one could avoid snakes by being careful around wooded areas, brush piles, stone walls, overgrown weedy patches, and abandoned outbuildings. Nothing suggested snakes might also lurk just outside the back door. The Virginia Poison Center recommends "if you see a snake, simply move slowly away from it." Nice advice. If you see the snake. My husband did not see it until after it had bitten him.

I grabbed my car keys. Ten minutes later we experienced the efficient care offered by Centra Southside Community Hospital's Emergency Department. Apparently a copperhead bite earns the victim immediate entrance to a treatment room for antivenom therapy followed by an overnight stay in intensive care. My husband says the bite starts out like a bad bee sting. And then, it gets worse. Much worse.

But, with prompt medical care, it also gets better. So, with a sigh of relief, we offer a big "Thank You" to the hospital staff and to all the people who have called with words of support and to trade snake stories.

And, just for the record, I'd like to add that the next time we have an open evening, my husband will NOT be permitted to organize the night's activities.

A FIELD OF TREES
March 2011

Have you heard the joke about the city slicker who bought a farm to raise chickens? It didn't go very well. He thinks he planted the chicks too deep.

Or, the one about the visiting urbanite who refused a breakfast with farm-fresh eggs? Her delicate palate would tolerate only eggs from the grocery store. She simply could not bring herself to eat the kind that came from the back end of a chicken.

If you haven't heard one of these, perhaps you've chuckled over a number of other farm jokes in which a clueless visitor couldn't tell a dog from a sheep or a horse from a cow. I've laughed over these, too. And, although I don't have an agricultural heritage, I didn't consider myself totally clueless. I knew that bread first grew in a field, and milk first grew in a cow (or, occasionally, a goat). I could even recognize corn on the stalk. Yes sir, I understood there was an intimate connection between what farmers did and what ended up on my dining room table.

But until I awoke one morning and heard the distant buzz of a saw, I never considered that the table itself was also an agricultural product. My table, and the chairs that go with it, came from a store in town. I love its warm, polished surface. When I bought it, I realized it was oak, but I never paused to consider that this was a kind of tree. The same kind of tree, in fact, that stands outside my dining room window.

Deep inside my brain, at a level unreached by everyday conscious thoughts, I knew that wood had an origin even farther back than a home improvement store or lumber yard. I knew it came from trees. But before moving here, I never really thought about the fact that trees were a crop—planted, cultivated, and harvested. The concept of farming in slow motion, nurturing plants over a generation instead of a year, was something I simply hadn't considered.

I should have had a clue. A few years before my husband and I decided to relocate here, we drove through the surrounding countryside. Somewhere up in Fluvanna County, we saw piles and piles of tree trunks stacked neatly beside a railroad track. I wondered where they had all come from and what they were for. But, I got distracted by the beauty of the countryside and forgot about them—until I heard the sounds associated with felling timber.

The trees near my home were harvested over a period of several weeks. During that time, I found myself constantly amazed by the number of wood products I had taken for granted. In addition to my table, there was my favorite rocking chair. My sofa. My desk. The secretary that I inherited from my grandmother's grandmother. A picture frame. Knife handles. Book cases. Wood, wood, wood. One day, with a shock of surprise, I realized the house itself was made of wood, too.

I decided to do a little research and was stunned to find out that the Commonwealth of Virginia comprises 25 million acres of land, and according to the most recent figures available from the Department of Forestry, 15.7 million of those acres are forested. That's more than half of the state (62%). And, 15.3 million of these forested acres are classified as commercial timberland.

I have certainly enjoyed Virginia's forests. They are magnificent. They provide places to wander and renew the spirit. They help keep the environment healthy by cleaning the air, purifying the water, and providing habitat for all kinds of wildlife. They are also managed crops. Planted, tended, grown, and harvested. Again, and again, and again.

I also discovered that the diversity of products related to trees is mind boggling. Yes, there's wood, which has the distinction of being the most utilized of all of America's raw materials. But there's also paper. Still other tree products are used in medications, spices, sandwich bags, adhesives, home decorating fabrics, tires, soft drinks, and even hot chocolate. And that's no joke.

HARVEST TIME
September 2011

Living in a place called Farmville and reading about the exploits of the local garden club inspired me to think that, yes, I could grow a plant. Admittedly, I have a bad track record. I've killed African violets, miniature roses, philodendron, ivy, jade, cyclamen, poinsettias, and even an entire dish garden full of cacti. This time would be different, and confidently I told my husband so.

Several mornings later, I woke to discover that he'd been to the garden center and purchased four baby tomato plants. Two were cherry tomatoes, one was an "early girl," and the other boasted it was a "better boy."

"Where do you want to plant them?" he asked, looking out over the backyard.

"Up here on the deck," I answered. "Away from the deer." I'd read about the hazards of local gardening, and I felt smug in my knowledge. "I've got some old flower pots we can use." Having thriving plants take up occupancy would erase the evidence of my past failures.

He looked at me the way a kindergarten teacher looks at a student when explaining that finger paints and paste aren't for eating. "You'll need something a lot bigger." He held his arms out as if he meant to hug an invisible Santa.

I looked back at the four little plants. "I wasn't planning on putting them in the same pot," I explained.

He confirmed, "You'll need four pots about this big." He indicated a size large enough to serve as a soup kettle for an entire village. Then he added, "And dirt."

I didn't understand what was wrong with the dirt we had in the yard, but I agreed to go to the store with him.

He located containers—huge plant tubs—available in red, green, and ivory. He let me pick the color. I evaluated the implications. Ivory was a bland color, and I was pretty certain my plants wanted something more vibrant. The red was vibrant, but I had enough fashion sense to realize that it can be hard to match reds. I didn't want that early girl to refuse to produce a tomato because it might clash with her pot. The green, however, would blend with the foliage, helping each ripe tomato stand out like a jewel. "Green," I said.

"We'll need some tomato cages, too," my husband said, picking up cones made of wire.

"Are they apt to wander off?" I asked.

His patience did not waver as he explained that they needed something to climb. I envisioned small tomatoes swinging on a jungle gym.

Back home, after my husband finished the planting, he invited me to inspect his handiwork. The tomatoes looked a little lonely—each plant inside such an enormous space. I wondered if they felt like people on rafts that had been washed out to sea. Could they even glimpse the horizons of their individual pots? But I kept those thoughts to myself. "They look great," I said.

And then the miracle happened. The baby plants hovered at the tiny stage for just a few days, and then they started dangling branches over the rungs of their cages, heaving themselves higher and higher. In a matter of weeks, their formerly huge tubs looked like shoes almost a size too small.

The cherry tomatoes blossomed first. Then, their yellow flowers gave way to green orbs hardly bigger than peas. They swelled, and two took on an orange hue. A couple days later, they turned bright red. I plucked them for dinner. I got out our best china, sliced both in half, and artfully arranged them on salad plates.

Those precursors heralded the arrival of grape-like clusters of cherry tomatoes. Then the early girl started yielding, and I made salads. I adorned pasta dishes. I made broiled tomatoes. I sliced fresh tomatoes for hamburgers.

The better boy hasn't yet lived up to his claims, but perhaps his time is still to come. I've got my fork and knife at the ready.

And I am glowing with satisfaction. I have finally learned the secret to cultivating plants: Let my husband do it.

GETTING THE WORM
June 2015

Everyone knows the early bird gets the worm. And people who know me, know that I am not an early bird. When it comes to morning and proverbs, I'm more suited to the saying, "The second mouse gets the cheese." But when it comes to yardwork, I've developed a new appreciation for worms.

Earthworms, with their long segmented bodies, are essentially eating machines. They eat their way through dirt. The mouth is at the beginning of the first segment. The anus is at the back end of the last. Most of the middle contains intestines, where the worm's food is digested. According to National Geographic, an individual worm can eat up to the equivalent of a third of its own body weight in dirt per day.

In Canada and some northern states where native worms were wiped out in the last ice age, the introduction of non-native worms is harming forest ecosystems. Here, however, and in many other agricultural communities, the presence of worms is actually an indicator of soil health.

Plants can't directly consume decomposing organic material in the soil, but worms can. After worms digest their dirt meals, worm castings (waste material) deliver nitrogen, calcium, magnesium, and phosphorus to the soil. These are nutrients plants can use. The U.S. Department of Agriculture claims that an acre of healthy land may contain as many as a million worms and those worms consume two tons of dirt per year.

Worms also help in other ways. The tunnels they dig aerate the soil and leave holes for plant roots to follow. When they carry their wastes from lower in the earth to the surface, they help promote useful microbial activity. And, when it rains, their burrows enable water to penetrate the ground rather than just running off.

None of these wormy benefits were originally present in my yard. My house in Farmville came with bright red Virginia clay—the stuff historians identified as being perfect for brickmaking. In colonial times, people made bricks by shaping this kind of clay in wooden forms and then baking it in kilns. The process that went into creating my yard was a little less formal. No one shaped the clay into pieces, and the baking was done naturally under the summer sun. Nevertheless, the results were pretty much the same, and apparently worms don't tunnel through brick.

It didn't take long for us to notice that our grass wasn't growing. Our weeds weren't even growing. When rain fell, rivulets gathered and coursed through our yard, leaving streaks of bare earth in their wake. We needed to do something to slow the water down, so we contacted the Virginia Cooperative Extension to get a soil test. It sounded simple enough. Step one, pick up a Soil Sample Box. Step two, dig up some dirt to put in the box. We had to resort to scratching and scraping up pieces of the hard clay, but we did manage to get a sample. The test results were hardly surprising. We needed to add lime and organic matter.

My husband set up a composting area, and he jokingly called it his dirt farm. We chopped up yard waste and grass clippings. We added old mulch. We added coffee grounds. He turned the mixture from time to time to aerate the pile. Eventually, it started to look like dirt, and he began incorporating it into patches of our yard.

Progress has been slow. In fact, it has taken several years, but now some of those patches serve as spots for gardening. This year, for the first time, we decided to plant some tomatoes in the ground instead of containers or raised beds. While we were digging one of the holes, the shovel turned over a lump of soil, and there wriggling atop the mound was a worm. An actual worm. We carefully patted it back into its subterranean home.

Now I've got a real dilemma. I may have to start getting up before the birds so that I can chase them off and protect my worm.

BE A SUPERHERO
July 2015

Usually it's only superheroes who get an opportunity to save the planet, but last month I had my chance. I didn't have to soar through the atmosphere with a jet pack or survive beneath a frozen sea. I didn't have to venture to an alternate dimension or even travel very far. I helped save the planet right here in Farmville. It took just a few hours one Saturday afternoon.

On June 6, 2015, seventeen people from several local organizations (including Friends of High Bridge Trail State Park, Friends of the Appomattox River, and Clean Virginia Waterways) worked together to pick up trash in and around Gross Creek, the narrow tributary that runs through town, east of Main Street. Over the course of three hours we waded through water, weeds, and muck and picked up all sorts of human detritus: plastic bags, bottles, paper plates, food wrappers, Styrofoam pieces, broken toys, and more. We bagged (literally) 800 pounds of trash. Not bad for an afternoon's haul.

How did this help save the planet? Gross Creek isn't just an isolated stretch of water. It empties into the Appomattox River, which in turn drains into the James River. The James River pours itself into the Chesapeake Bay near the edge of the Atlantic. Every piece of litter we picked up did not get washed downstream, did not find its way into the Chesapeake Bay, and did not end up in the planet's interconnected marine environments.

Large pieces of marine debris are an eyesore and can damage aquatic habitats. Tiny pieces can end up in the food chain through the stomachs of birds, fish, and other aquatic animals. Pieces of all sizes provide substrate for the transportation of invasive species that can wreak havoc on fisheries and ecosystems.

One of the biggest problems is actually one of the hardest to see. Once trash—especially plastic—enters the ocean, wave action and sunlight combine to break it into smaller and smaller pieces. The National Oceanic and Atmospheric Administration (NOAA) describes the resulting mix as a kind of "peppery soup" suspended in the water column. This type of particulate debris builds up in the centers of gigantic surface ocean currents called gyres. The accumulation in the northern Pacific, called the Great Pacific Garbage Patch, is perhaps the most infamous, but similar areas exist in all Earth's oceans.

Cleaning up will be a major—perhaps even insurmountable—task. Some experts claim operating the number of ships required to do the job would likely cause more environmental damage than would be mitigated. Furthermore, filtering microscopic particles out of seawater could destroy vast amounts of phytoplankton, and phytoplankton photosynthesis creates half of the world's oxygen. One of the most innovative proposals comes from Boyan Slat, a 20-year-old from the Netherlands, who is working to deploy a massive debris collection system, but even his best-case scenarios won't be enough if we keep adding more trash to the oceans.

In light of the problem's enormity, you may be wondering how picking up a mere 800 pounds of litter could help. That effort was part of a larger project called Clean the Bay Day, an annual event undertaken by the Chesapeake Bay Foundation (http://www.cbf.org). On that same afternoon, 6,000 volunteers worked throughout the Chesapeake Bay Watershed at 275 different sites. The day's catch totaled 105,000 pounds of trash. Since 1989, 140,000 Clean the Bay Day volunteers have collected 6.2 million pounds of trash. It does all add up.

Ironically, most of the trash we picked up seemed to be picnic leftovers, stuff lost or left behind by people who were out presumably to enjoy the beauty of nature. If you find yourself at a picnic this summer, you can help save the planet by making sure your trash ends up in appropriate receptacles. If you want to do more, Clean Virginia Waterways will be hosting clean up events this fall. And, the Chesapeake Bay Foundation organizes Clean the Bay Day annually. Keep your eyes open for your opportunity to participate. You can be a superhero, too.

HAPPY TRAILS TO YOU
June 2010

My husband and I are frequent bikers along the High Bridge Trail State Park. Maybe you've seen us. He's the sleek, handsome one gliding along effortlessly with smooth, strong strokes. I'm the short, fat one peddling hard and puffing. He is a mountain bike enthusiast who has acquiesced to the tame terrain available locally. I'm a biking novice. In fact, until I saw the smooth surface and barely perceptible hills of the High Bridge Trail, the possibility of exercise on wheels held no appeal to me at all. None.

Now I'm hooked.

You'll find me out on the trail about three times a week. Last year, when I first started riding, my route was a modest two-mile loop from the River Road parking lot out to High Bridge and back. It wasn't long before I could do it twice for a total of four miles.

My next milestone was conquering the route from the River Road parking lot to the Osborne Road parking lot and back—six miles. This route covers one of the most scenic stretches of the trail. There are places where the old rail bed is high above the surrounding countryside, and there are places where it was cut through hills, creating the effect of riding through canyons.

By starting from the Osborne Road parking lot and continuing all the way out to High Bridge, I expanded my route to eight miles. Then, I added a loop at the end of my ride by pressing on to the trailhead at Main Street before turning around and returning to the parking lot. I was at nine miles. Tacking the loop to Main Street on to the beginning of my ride as well as the end put me at ten miles. Double digits. I felt the thrill of accomplishment.

It was time for bigger things, so I set my sights to the west. Beginning in Farmville, a loop to the Tuggle Road parking lot at the Hardtimes Road intersection and back is about 11 miles.

My current favorite route is a 12-mile loop. I begin in town, head west, continue a little way past Hardtimes Road, then I turn around and come back. The westbound six miles of this route are my biggest challenge. Although my husband doesn't even notice the grade, I can attest to the fact that heading west from Farmville is an uphill journey. It is a gradual, gentle incline, but it is steady. I call it the long wind-up. When I get to the end of those six miles, my legs and lungs are spent. But then comes the reward. Six miles of a smooth trail with a friendly grade—downhill. I can fly. The wind. The freedom. The exhilaration. I return to my starting point, renewed.

There are other paths, other parking lots, other starting points. I have ridden from Hardtimes Road to Prospect. I have ridden from Prospect to the trail's end in Pamplin. And, I'm looking forward to the day when I can ride farther east, including a stretch across High Bridge itself. (This portion of the trail didn't open until 2012.)

I have met people on the trail who have come from Charlottesville, Lynchburg, and other distant places to enjoy it. But I have also encountered neighbors who haven't yet ventured forth. If you haven't yet set foot or wheel on High Bridge Trail, today could be the perfect opportunity. I hope to see you there.

⇒ AROUND TOWN   91

WHAT'S ON TV TONIGHT?
April 2011

Last month the Nielsen company sent me information claiming I had been specially selected to participate in a survey about television viewing habits. They said my answers would help determine what you, my neighbors and fellow Farmvillians, watch on television.

I am supposed to be pleased about being selected, but I was stunned. I am utterly unqualified for this honor.

Nevertheless, I read through the literature and checked the Nielson website to find some facts about typical viewing habits. I learned that the average number of televisions per household is 2.5. My husband and I come fairly close to this. We have two, one in the living room and one in the exercise room. I also found out that the overwhelming majority of homes with a television (about 95%) have a DVD player. So far, we seemed pretty close to normal.

Then, the Nielson statistics went on to claim that the average American watches his or her televisions for a total of 35.6 hours per week. I did the math. This is approximately five hours per day, and as best as I could determine they meant hours spent watching broadcast programming. My thin veneer of normalcy evaporated entirely.

The last broadcast television program I watched in my own home was the finale to the series *M*A*S*H*. It aired in 1983. Because it seemed like a culturally relevant event, my husband and I cleaned out a closet to locate our portable black and white set. Back then, the set's rabbit ears were all you needed to tune in. I don't remember how long the show was, but it may have been an hour. If so, that puts my average viewing of television broadcasts for the past 28 years at about two minutes a year.

This doesn't mean I haven't encountered television broadcasts. Televisions crop up everywhere—restaurants, waiting rooms, gas stations, banks, and even the car next to yours driving down Third Street. But these exposures haven't shown me anything I'd want to watch on purpose.

For example, a couple weeks ago, I had to spend some time in several medical waiting rooms (I'm all better now; thanks for asking). I saw part of a program where brides said unkind things about each others' weddings. I saw part of a program where a dog trainer tried to get his canine pupil to walk on a treadmill. I saw advertisements for an upcoming program about making a dress out of cupcakes. Shows such as these are marketed as "reality" shows, but they misuse the term. Reality is when you go to your nephew's wedding and hug the bride. Reality is when you walk your own dog, learn to make your own dress, or best of all, bake and eat your cupcakes.

Based on these limited experiences, I was able to answer the first question in my television viewing survey: How do I rate the quality of today's TV programming? Not at all satisfied. The next question was fairly easy: What do I typically watch? Rented or purchased DVDs. In fact, my husband and I often celebrate the arrival of Friday night by spending a couple hours watching a movie. We get two a month from Netflix, we occasionally borrow one from the library, and we have a collection of favorites we've watched over and over again. Our own version of reruns.

I ran into trouble on question three. How many working television sets are in my home? They underlined the word working. We do have two televisions. Technically, they both work. But neither is connected to an antenna, satellite dish, or cable so they don't receive broadcast programming.

This glitch may mean that the Nielson company will disregard my input. Perhaps they will pay more attention to someone else—someone who has more intense experience with the slate of currently offered television shows. But if they do retract their offer to let me play a role in deciding what others watch on television, I won't mind being ignored. I'll be out and about enjoying my own version of reality, and I hope to see you there.

NOT "NOTHING TO DO"
October 2011

I'm a lucky parent. My children, who all live in other states, seem to like visiting me. Two of them live in large cities—not in the suburbs, but amid the traffic and neon, right on the corner of Hustle and Bustle. The third lives just an hour's train ride from Manhattan, a place famous for never sleeping.

They're all used to a lot of activity. But when they show up here, my favorite thing to do is sit down and visit on the back porch, sip iced tea, watch the birds, and listen to the neighbor's cows mooing. I suppose my kids can be forgiven for reaching the incorrect conclusion that I live a quiet (possibly even boring) life and that there's nothing to do in Farmville.

The truth is exactly the opposite. Farmville teems with things to do. So much so, that it's a rare day when I do get to sit and listen to those cows.

There are the big community-wide events like The Heart of Virginia Festival and First Fridays. Then there are churches, clubs, and volunteer organizations and their attendant meetings and events. Along with all these things are a host of entertainments and educational offerings at Longwood University and Hampden-Sydney College. If you haven't yet taken advantage of any of these, you may be surprised to find that the price of admission is surprisingly low—frequently free—and the performers and speakers are often internationally known celebrities in their fields.

Since moving to Farmville, I've enjoyed a wide variety of music including performances by jazz bands, orchestras, and small chamber groups. I have been to vocal concerts, listened to classical music that has been loved for centuries, and been privileged to hear innovative pieces being performed publicly for the first time. I discovered I have a weakness for bluegrass and, surprisingly, a favorite pianist—Christopher O'Riley, who performed at Longwood University last month. What he did with the 88 keys on a single piano was nothing short of magic. I am still in awe.

Speaking of magic, Lancer Productions sponsored a performance by an illusionist last spring that was astounding and hilarious. But everything to do around town isn't just for fun. The schools, along with other organizations, also offer lectures and forums. Over the past couple years, I've learned about China's role in the world and how New York's big publishers design book covers. I have watched historical presentations, listened to experts discuss interfaith reconciliation, and learned about our nation's efforts to overcome a legacy of racial injustices. I even attended my first opera.

Literature is something that is important to me. In Farmville, I've met authors, discussed books, and started a collection of signed copies. I've attended plays and musicals at LU and HSC, and I've discovered what a gem the community has in the Waterworks Theater. Before moving to Farmville, I'd never seen a British pantomime. Now, I can't imagine Christmas without one, and I'm already wondering what they've got in store for this year. But I don't need to wait until then to see what else the Waterworks crew is concocting. This month, they are presenting the musical *Chicago*. I'll be there.

If all this is starting to sound like stuffy indoor stuff, don't forget that the High Bridge Trail State Park comes right through downtown. In addition, Bear Creek Lake State Park, Holliday Lake State Park, Sailor's Creek Battlefield State Park, and Twin Lakes State Park are all within easy driving distance. I have enjoyed walking through forests, hiking around lakes, and biking past historical sites. Last summer, I even finally got a chance to try my hand at kayaking. And, yes, I had a great time.

So if you host an event, and I'm not there, it isn't because I didn't want to come. It's only that I can't figure out how to be in all the places I'd like to be at the same time. Either that, or I'm sitting out on the back porch with one of my children. And that's the most precious event of all.

FOR THE FIRST TIME
March 2012

I remember the first time I set foot on High Bridge Trail State Park. At that time, in the spring of 2009, only the first few miles were open. My husband and I walked from the River Road parking lot out to the edge of High Bridge itself—about a mile. We watched birds. We glimpsed cows in a distant pasture. The fresh air and sunshine were perfect remedies for our winter-weary souls.

A fence blocked access to the bridge itself, and a sign promised future development. A picnic table provided a spot for gazing at the Appomattox River valley through chain links and resting before beginning the walk back to the car.

Although I am not an athletic person, I do enjoy ambling among trees and under the sun. My husband, a perfect gentleman, has accompanied me through uncounted miles without so much as the hint of a grumble, even though I know his true passion for the outdoors involves a more vigorous approach.

He has long been an enthusiastic bike rider. His favorite brand of riding is called mountain biking. As best as I can tell, the object is to take a bicycle up the side of a mountain and fling yourself off its peak. On the way down, you bounce off rocks and roots, collecting bruises and blazing a trail by leaving hunks of skin behind. When you get to the bottom, you can tell how much fun you had by the quantity of blood lost.

My own bike-related activities officially ended sometime around fifth grade when I learned it was safer to beg a ride in a car than compete with one for a few inches of asphalt. The closest adult experience I had to biking involved a piece of exercise equipment that required hunching over handlebars until my wrists and back ached. So, despite my husband's willingness to walk with me, I never reciprocated and rode with him.

Then one day, we met a couple riding a style of bike that enabled them to sit upright. They called these "comfort" bikes. My eyes were opened. I noted the trail's flat grade and utter lack of precipices. I saw its even, crushed stone surface. I whispered, "I could ride a bike on this." Eager to help me embrace even a small part of something he loved, my husband bought me a bike.

My first ride was from the River Road access parking lot out to the bridge. Within a week, I could easily do two laps. Then we started riding between the Osborne Road and River Road parking lots, six miles. We added the extension to Main Street, seven miles.

As High Bridge Trail State Park opened new sections, we explored. We have ridden from Farmville to the Tuggle Road intersection and beyond. We have embarked from Prospect and from Rice. We have ridden to the Park's western terminus in Pamplin and to its eastern terminus near Burkeville. My typical ride is now 15 miles, and once I rode 20.

The only part of High Bridge Trail State Park's 31 miles I hadn't experienced at the time this column was originally written was crossing the bridge itself. But the time for doing just that was approaching.

A First-to-Cross contest offered by The Friends of High Bridge Trail State Park promised one lucky person the opportunity to be the first official park visitor to cross the newly rehabilitated bridge. The winner was chosen in a drawing on March 11, 2012 at Charley's Waterfront Cafe.

I had a stack of tickets. When the winning stub was drawn, it wasn't mine. Someone else got the honor. I didn't lose, however. The Park opened the Bridge in April 2012, and I finally received my chance, my first time to cross High Bridge.

MY JOURNEY OF A THOUSAND MILES
May 2014

By the time you read this, I'll have 1,000 miles on my bicycle. When I got home from my most recent bike ride, the odometer said 998.6 miles. I know just where I'm going to go to get the 1.4 miles that will take me over the top into the new world of four-digit numbers. If I begin in the River Road parking lot for High Bridge Trail State Park, I'll rack up 0.9 miles to get to High Bridge and then another 0.5 miles to cross it. Do the math. I'll reach 1,000 miles just as I finish crossing the bridge.

It seems a fitting stage for such an accomplishment. When I first started riding a bike, my route took me from that very same parking lot to a chain link fence that blocked access to the bridge itself. A sign promised future development. I remember the many times I stopped there to catch my breath, gaze out over the valley, and turn around. A couple of years later, the fence came down.

My first bike trip across High Bridge was a bit terrifying. The barrier that guards the sides of the bridge stands nearly as high as I am tall. On foot, I had to look through it. On my bike, I saw over the top. Suddenly, there appeared to be nothing between me and the great beyond—or, rather, the great below. It took a few crossings before I felt comfortable, but then I started enjoying the view. The stretch of treetops passing beneath me. The open expanse above me. The distant hills. The river running below my feet.

At this point, I don't know how many crossings I've completed. I don't even know how many miles are actually on my bike because the odometer wasn't original equipment. I added it when I upgraded the shifter and brakes. But those documented miles seem to possess a reality that earlier miles lack, and although I've accumulated them on many different sections of the trail, I feel a special affinity for the bridge itself.

The bridge and I have both been through major transformations during our lives, and we've both suffered the indignities of aging. The original High Bridge was built in 1853. Its trusses were reinforced with arches a few years later. It hosted battles in 1865, and part of it was burned. It was fixed. Then in 1886, it was refurbished. And again in 1901. By 1913, its original brick piers had deteriorated to the point where they couldn't just be patched again, so the bridge was rebuilt with steel towers. It carried heavier trains. It served faithfully for decades, and then it was abandoned. Now, reclaimed and resurrected, it enjoys new life as the longest pedestrian bridge in Virginia.

My own journey into the present began with a long stint where I labored in an office in front of a computer screen for sixty or more hours a week. My body deteriorated. I battled pain. I experienced injuries that made it difficult to walk or even to stand. I was crumbling. My feet required fixing, and I needed arch supports. Finally, I rebuilt my life to make time for physical activities. Now, repurposed, I enjoy days with periods set aside to pursue fitness, fresh air, and sunshine.

Yet, despite these improvements, the years have yielded unchangeable alterations. High Bridge no longer hefts freight and passenger trains. Instead, it carries people on foot, bicyclists, and horses. And me, I've abandoned hopes for a svelte body. I'm settling for the one I've got. I still carry the excess weight it took a lifetime to accumulate, and I get winded when I face the tiny swells that count as hills along the trail's essentially flat expanse. I may never ride from Pamplin to Burkeville in one excursion. In fact, I'm still working my way back up to distances that were routine for me at the end of last year's riding season.

But 1,000 miles. For me and for the bridge that has carried so many others on their journeys, that's something to celebrate.

INTO THE FUTURE
May 2016

Congratulations to this year's graduates. Longwood University, Hampden-Sydney College, and Southside Virginia Community College will all host ceremonies this month to celebrate the successes of students who have earned postsecondary degrees, honors, and other credentials. Area high schools will mark the achievements of their own graduates by conferring diplomas, and various academies of dance, music, and martial arts will mark the end of a year's accomplishments with performances, competitions, and advancements.

The observances of these events will employ various symbols. Some participants will wear traditional regalia. They may receive hoods or toss special hats into the air. They may move tassels to signify a change in their academic status. Some will receive flowers, emblems, or applause. Some will laugh. Some will cry. But all will be changed as one stage of life and learning yields to another.

In *Mere Christianity*, C. S. Lewis noted, "It may be hard for an egg to turn into a bird: it would be a jolly sight harder for it to learn to fly while remaining an egg. We are like eggs at present. And you cannot go on indefinitely being just an ordinary, decent egg. We must be hatched or go bad."

The rites of formal education are replete with strategically planned hatchings, but life also serves up abundant opportunities for transformation to individual people, to communities, and to nations.

During a recent walk through Farmville's downtown area, I was struck by how much had changed since I first moved to the community. It's been seven years. To me, it seems as if those years passed in a blink, but apparently it was an eventful blink. Stores and eateries have come and gone. Façades have been updated. Display windows have been dressed and redressed. The downtown plaza area at the entrance to High Bridge Trail State Park didn't used to exist, but now it is a flowering showcase.

Over a longer period of time, the community's spirit and attitude have apparently also changed and blossomed. Historically, Farmville endured a period of time marked by racial tension and discrimination. Many of the people I meet today are embarrassed by the ignorance of elder days. They've learned from history and grown beyond its limitations. They have graduated into an enlarged understanding of the human family and how each individual is interwoven into the fabric of society. The community, once divided over racial issues, moves on and embraces cooperation and respect.

Sometimes change comes quickly. Sometimes changes emerge from longer processes, and important turning points may go unrecognized when they occur. Several weeks ago, I attended a Bible study where we discussed a passage in the Gospel of John that mentioned how Jesus's disciples did not understand the significance of the events they witnessed until much later (John 12:16). It brought to my mind a program I once attended at Sailor's Creek Battlefield State Park. That presentation included readings from Civil War era diaries. Entries had been recorded by people who observed battles but didn't understand what they had seen.

And I wondered: What turning points are occurring right now? What events that currently seem ordinary will unleash extraordinary consequences? Who among us will lead us to achievements we can't yet imagine?

Perhaps a teacher is setting a future scientist on the path to discovery. Perhaps a student volunteer is developing a passion for social justice that will transform the next generation. Perhaps an older person is sharing wisdom that will ultimately produce an abundant harvest among those in whom it takes root.

I've been watching signs around town as the past winter changed to spring and as spring transitions into summer. People who once huddled indoors have taken to their yards. Seeds have been planted. Gardens are being nurtured. Students formerly cocooned in scarves and jackets are now attired in shorts and sandals. Some are ready to fly away for the summer. Others will fly off to uncharted destinations.

So to all the classes of 2016—and to everyone else with potential yet to be realized—I wish you a fruitful journey into the future.

BETTER EDUCATION
November 2011

Last month I had the privilege of attending the Community Banquet for the Robert Russa Moton Museum. The keynote speaker was Edward Lewis, founder of Essence Communications—the publisher of *Essence Magazine*, a host of other accomplishments, and cousin to Barbara Rose Johns.

If you're from Farmville, you probably already know the story: In 1951, Johns led her fellow students in a walkout to protest their woefully inadequate school. The student strike helped to bring the plight of African American students to our nation's consciousness. The legal battle that ensued became one of five cases incorporated into *Brown v. Board of Education*, the case by which the U.S. Supreme Court ruled against segregation in schools.

Mr. Lewis's telling of the story was enlightening and inspiring. It was delivered to a standing-room-only crowd, including many who had been directly touched by the events he described. One of the night's opportunities was for each attending person to fill out a card describing how he or she had personally been impacted.

As a newcomer to the area, I felt that the story wasn't mine. The initial student protest happened several years prior to my birth. I thought that the events that happened here hadn't touched me at all. I left my card on the table, blank.

Since then, I've had time to reflect, and I was surprised to discover that I do indeed have a small piece of the story to tell:

My family moved around a lot while I was growing up. As a result, I attended a total of six different schools in four states. Fourth grade found me living in a small town on Virginia's Eastern Shore. My fourth grade class was all white. Perhaps some of my fellow fourth graders were aware of this fact, but at the time I didn't think about it. I had a playmate who lived across the street from me. She was the only girl my age within walking distance of my home, so we spent a lot of time together. She was African American, and she went to a different school. I once had another friend who attended a Catholic school, so to my fourth-grade mentality it didn't seem all that odd that neighbors would go to different schools.

But during the summer between my fourth and fifth grades, the schools in the Eastern Shore made plans to integrate. My friend and I were excited by the thought that we could go to the same school together. Our excitement was short lived, however, when a house fire forced her family to relocate. Years later, I related this story to someone, and they asked if the fire had occurred under suspect circumstances. I hope not, but in truth I don't know. Those kinds of suspicions simply were not part of my awareness.

But fifth grade was still an adventure with a lot of new people to meet. I especially remember a young man by the name of Drexel who was assigned a seat directly in front of me. He had a quick smile and warm, dark eyes. Any excuse to whisper to him, I took. In retrospect, I suppose I might have been flirting. The teacher had a standard punishment for talking in class. The offender had to stay inside during recess and write "I must not talk in class" a hundred times. By the year's end, I'd been on the receiving end of this penalty so often I had developed the skill of holding three pencils in my hand so that I could write three lines at a time.

I can't say how things ultimately turned out at that school. My family moved on. But after fourth grade, I never again attended a segregated school. For this good fortune, I now know I can thank a group of students from Farmville who were bold enough to stand up against inequity. Because of their efforts, I received a better education than I might have otherwise. And, currently, I'm proud to be part of a community that remembers the legacy of its past while striving toward a brighter future.

HAS IT BEEN SUCH A LONG TIME?
August 2013

I've reached a milestone. The first column I wrote for *The Farmville Herald* appeared in August 2009, so this one officially begins my fifth year.

In some ways, it feels like I've been here a long time. I remember when the local custom of using historical references for locations left me confused. People would say, "You know, the corner where the old bank used to be." Or, "That development where the Safeway was."

Although it took me a while to learn my way around using reference points that don't still exist, I've got them located now. I even acquired the habit of referring to places no longer on the map. During one bike ride, a man I stopped to chat with asked, "Do you know where that new bike rental shop is?" Yes, I did. Without hesitation, I replied, "It's where Rug Rats used to be before they moved." I saw his eyes light with recognition. He knew exactly where I meant.

Emboldened, I mentioned to someone that I'd now lived here a long time. She laughed and shook her head. She'd moved to Farmville 35 years ago. She didn't need to make a mental note about where the Safeway used to be; she remembered the actual store. "Town used to end right after that," she told me. "Past where McDonald's is, there was nothing." Furthermore, she didn't think her 35 years qualified as a long time. I considered the length of her years in Farmville compared to events in my own life. Thirty-five years ago, I did not have any children. I hadn't even yet met my husband. That wasn't just a long time ago, it was a lifetime ago.

But then I thought about her 35 years in the context of events in the area's history, and I had to agree that a span of 35 years was a mere blink. It was only fifty years ago that students were arrested in Farmville for trying to integrate church services. And only 62 years ago, Barbara Johns led her peers on a strike for equality in education. Diligent efforts at racial reconciliation continue, but apparently the timeframe for complete healing hasn't yet been fulfilled.

So, if time frames of fifty and sixty years could seem short, I wondered what might constitute a truly long time.

I've been to events describing the final days of the Civil War as it marched through town nearly 150 years ago. That seemed like a long time ago—until I learned that Patrick Henry served on the Hampden-Sydney College Board of Trustees around the time our nation was born. Compared with the 1770s, the Civil War suddenly seemed quite recent. But, Henry himself was born more than a century after the first European settlers arrived at Jamestown. That year, 1607, I thought was certainly a long time ago.

Then I recalled a talk given by Longwood University's Dr. Jim Jordan. Apparently the Native Americans who greeted the first English colonists were recent arrivals themselves. Dr. Jordan described his work at an archeological dig that uncovered settlements near Buffalo Creek—settlements that dated back a couple thousand years. Within that context, our nation's entire history seemed just a moment.

My perspective on what might constitute a long time received another challenge when I signed up for the Virginia Master Naturalist program. In a class about the geological history of the Piedmont, I learned about mountain formation and the continental rifting process that opened up an ocean. Within that context, the entire scope of human history—with all its political schemes, violence, and tragedies and all its hopes and aspirations—amounted to just a single tick on the global clock.

For a moment, I felt insignificant and overwhelmed by the seeming pointlessness of it all. But then my perspective shifted, and I saw it in a different way: How much people have accomplished in such a short time and how much I've come to love Farmville in just a few short years. I've only been here a brief moment, but what a moment it's been! And I'm looking forward to my next milestone, whatever it may be.

LEARNING THE LINGO
April 2014

One gentle day I said, "I'm going to open a window." But when I said "window," instead of saying "win-doe," I heard myself say "win-duh." The utterance made me smile. I was learning to speak the language of Farmville.

During my childhood days, my family moved around a lot. I was always the new kid who talked funny. I became a linguistic chameleon. Without any real conscious effort and usually within the span of just a couple months, I'd acquire the new patois and merge my words seamlessly with my peers' chatter. I entered adulthood on Long Island where I spoke Long Islandese. From there, I found my way to Michigan. My boss in Michigan commanded me to speak properly. No problem. I was well practiced and apparently still pliable.

My adult years were unlike my experience growing up as a vagabond. I stayed put for decades. That Michigan accent now seems to be a permanent part of me. Permanent, but not altogether unyielding.

In Michigan, carbonated soft drinks are called "pop." "Soda" was the word I knew from my youth, and switching back to that term was fairly simple. My habit of ordering "iced tea" when dining out proved to be a greater challenge. It took me the better part of five years to remember to ask for "unsweet."

I've also occasionally been heard to say I was "fixin to do" something rather than "planning to do" it. And, in giving directions, I now know the proper location is "down the road a piece." "Down the road a bit" can be confused with "just a bitty bit," which isn't quite as far. I haven't yet said "y'all," when addressing an individual person, but I did once ask a group "What do all y'all think?" I don't remember what they thought, but no one seemed to notice that I'd said anything out of the ordinary.

Then there's the whole business of heart blessing. The first time I heard someone say, "Bless her heart," I was on a flight from Raleigh to Denver. I had an aisle seat from which I observed a diminutive woman wheel a large piece of luggage behind her. I wondered how she'd managed to smuggle the monstrosity past the gate agents. She found her seat but was unable to heft the bag into the overhead bin. She asked a flight attendant for help. After a struggle, another flight attendant was summoned. They finally succeeded in stowing the luggage and getting the woman belted into her seat. Then the two flight attendants walked away with smiles plastered across their faces. As they passed my seat I heard one say to the other, "Well, bless her heart."

I was amazed at such charity. Later during the flight, I observed these same flight attendants interacting with other passengers, and I was confused because at times they seemed downright surly. The incongruity of what I had observed and heard remained a mystery to me for several years.

Since then, I've had the opportunity to hear a lot of people bless the hearts of others. I now know it's used as a secret code for declaring, "What an idiot!" In truth, there are a lot of substitutes for the word "idiot" that are probably more accurate, but they aren't fit to print in a family newspaper. But, confusingly, at least for a non-native speaker, I've also heard the phrase uttered in a way that seemed sincere, flowing from the apparently genuine admiration of a benevolent act. I conclude that there must be some nuance of expression or context that yet eludes me.

Despite these small steps I've made toward learning the local lingo, I know I still speak like a midwesterner. And even if I acquire the habit of uttering an apt phrase or two, the words will probably always sound harsh to southern ears. Nevertheless, it is unlikely that I'll learn to hush my mouth, even given a month of Sundays. I'll continue to blunder along making inadvertent, and perhaps even amusing, linguistic faux pas. All I can say is, well, bless my heart.

URBAN VS. RURAL LIVING
October 2014

I participate in a book club that meets monthly at the Farmville-Prince Edward County Community Library. A while back, we read Steven Johnson's *The Ghost Map*, and I can't get it out of my mind.

Three-quarters of the book recounts the efforts of medical and political authorities working to contain a cholera epidemic that struck London during the mid-nineteenth century. The tale follows the efforts of Dr. John Snow and clergyman Henry Whitehead as they gathered scientific evidence in the face of overwhelming tragedy. Within the span of just a few days, the disease left virtually every family in one neighborhood bereaved. The story has all the intrigue and dramatic twists of a good mystery.

But the author didn't leave his story in the past, and that's the part that still troubles me. Johnson projected his inferences into the present and the future. If he had concluded that living in crowded, urban settings posed significant health challenges, I would have simply nodded my head in agreement and closed the book. I may have even recommended it.

Instead, Johnson summed up his book by making the seemingly contrary claim that—despite the challenges—living in a city was advantageous, actually preferable to living in a rural area. He offered this opinion as if it were a demonstrable fact rather than a personal lifestyle choice. Citing the benefits of multiculturalism, the early adoption of innovative technologies, and a purported smaller ecological footprint, he wrapped up his book by proclaiming that an urban lifestyle was morally superior to a rural one.

That assertion certainly raised my hackles. I specifically decided to move to Farmville because it was not an urban area. Many of my neighbors and new friends have also elected to come here or to remain here to avoid the various plagues of city life.

Admittedly, the rivalry between city and country has been running for nearly as long as the human record exists. People have often migrated from the countryside to seek opportunities in cities. The trend continues, especially in difficult economic times. The most recent U.S. Census reported a shrinking rural population. But to hear a city dweller smugly assert that people belonged in cities and not the country was not just unsettling. It was maddening.

I'll concede the point that people in densely packed urban areas experience some benefits rural folks miss. They have more options for medical care and public transportation. They have better access to new technology and enjoy a plethora of entertainment choices. Cultural artifacts like museums, symphonies, and statues sit at their doorsteps. They can even casually sample the feasts and festivals of people with roots in widely divergent traditions.

But in many cases, those celebrated roots and ethnic identities were forged in the fields and farms of the countryside. Far from being merely colorful reminders of days gone by, the customs of diverse groups represent the achievements of communities who had to cooperate to survive. The ways of life, norms, and habits encoded in ethnic identities matured as generations joined hands to grow crops, protect herds, and secure homes.

Cities can be nice places to visit, but their residents miss out on things a rural populace takes for granted. For example, green spaces can be hard to find in cities. And at night, if you look up to the stars, you might see one or two, but the glare of artificial lights will blind you to the marvels overhead. The practice of dwelling in cities fosters a misperception that human endeavors are substantial, maybe even permanent. Rural folk know better, and they have learned to respect nature and the immensity of the earth and the sky. Although engineering marvels like sky-scraper lined streets may be impressive, they fall far short of even the simplest of nature's wonders.

As a relative newcomer to a rural lifestyle, perhaps I haven't yet earned the right to be offended by crass pro-urbanism. After all, I'm still struggling to grow a small garden. Nevertheless, I'd like to affirm the intrinsic value of a lifestyle that prizes things like nature and perspective above technology and noise.

FARMVILLE, THAT'S WHERE I LIVE
August 2015

When my husband and I tell people from other places that we live in Farmville, their reactions are typically based on one of two basic assumptions. None guesses that Farmville is the true name of an actual place.

One group thinks we're joking. The year we moved to Farmville was the same year Zynga released its popular social network game, Farm-Ville. So, some people think I say I live in Farmville to indicate that I spend most of my waking hours at the computer sowing digital crops and milking avatars of cows. People who hold this misperception often feel disappointed when I confess that I've never played the game.

Another group tends to interpret the name metaphorically. Their confusion is understandable. The practice of naming towns with the suffix -ville (which is from the French word for village) was apparently popular in the United States' post-revolution era. A hundred years later, at least according to *The Oxford English Dictionary*, sports writers adopted a similar method for coining allegorical terms. They told their readers about baseball players from "sluggersville" and victors from "winnersville." By the 1970s, business reporters had also embraced the practice, and they wrote about figurative places called "marketville" and "mediaville."

Recently, I discovered that the name of our community here in Virginia isn't unique. There's also a Farmville in North Carolina. Farmville, VA and Farmville, NC seem to share a lot in common. For example, from the website of North Carolina's town (http://www.farmville-nc.com/), I learned that its Farmville has a settlement history that dates back to the latter half of the 1700s. The town features a blend of historic homes and newer communities, boasts of its support for the arts, and takes pride in a distinctive Main Street.

I began to wonder about other towns where our nation's agricultural history and heritage were made manifest in town names based on Farm-this and Farm-that. To satisfy my curiosity, I paged through a road atlas and opened Google Maps on my computer.

Although I found only the two communities in Virginia and North Carolina with the precise name Farmville, some others were remarkably close. Louisiana has a Farmerville, and seven states have towns called Farmersville (Alabama, California, Illinois, Indiana, Missouri, Ohio, and Texas). New York has a Farmersville Station.

In addition, farms, farmers, and farming featured prominently in place names without the -ville ending. I found two towns simply designated Farmer (North Carolina and Ohio), Farmer's Branch (Texas), Farmer City (Illinois), and Farmer's Valley (Pennsylvania). I also noticed Farmland (Indiana) and Farming (Minnesota).

Suffixes other than -ville were common. The ending -burg, for example, is a Scottish variation of the word borough (which refers to a town). I found one Farmersburg in Indiana and another in Iowa. A slightly more popular suffix was -dale (referring to a valley or area surrounded by hills). I found six U.S. towns named Farmingdale: Illinois, Maine, New Jersey, New York, South Dakota, and Vermont. The most popular suffix, however, was the one based on the word town, -ton. I found thirty (that's right, 30) states with places named Farmington. In other words, more than half of the states in the United States have a town (or other type of municipality) named Farmington.

I identified only twelve states that did not have a town name that started with "farm." One of them was Alaska. I suppose the Alaskan growing season is too short to crow about fields and farms. Nevada was another. I did find a couple of that state's towns named with the words "acres" and "field": Gold Acres and Goldfield. Presumably, Nevada's early settlers planned to cultivate something other than vegetables.

But, here in Farmville, VA, I find constant reminders our area's—and indeed, our nation's—agricultural heritage. Cows in the fields. Recently mown hay. Corn. Acres and acres of trees grown as crops. I also see a town abuzz with activity, boasting a university, a college, historic sites, modern neighborhoods, a vibrant arts community, and a beautiful, store-lined Main Street. Farmville. I'm proud to tell people that's where I live.

NATURAL TREASURES IN THE SKY OVERHEAD

September 2009

One recent night, I stepped out my front door and stood amazed at the glory of the night sky. The black celestial ceiling was studded with countless stars. The diffused glow of the Milky Way made a complete arch stretching from Sagittarius low in the south, passing through Cygnus high overhead, and descending toward the northern horizon as the lazy W of Cassiopeia rose into view.

It was a sky filled with wonder and mystery. It filled me with gratitude for the specialness of Earth's tiny corner in the vast universe. It connected me to history as I thought about earlier generations who have looked up into the same heavens. I considered the marvel and magnitude of God's handiwork.

I wanted to wake my neighbors and shout, "Come and see! Before it's too late," because such a night sky is an endangered treasure.

In many suburban areas, a glimpse of even a tiny portion of the Milky Way is a rarity. The overhead dome never gets really black, only grey. Against the competing sprawl of misdirected and reflected light only a small percentage of the night's heavenly bodies still twinkle. In cities, the man-made haze of light pollution routinely obscures all but the moon and a few of the brightest objects. Imagine what it means to be able to count the stars in the sky on one hand.

Here in south-central Virginia, a lot of the night sky is still fairly dark because distance protects it from billboards, shopping centers, and ill-aimed security lamps. But even here, the black of night is losing its battle. From my front porch, I don't need a map to see where the major shopping areas in Farmville are located. All I need do is look to the horizon and find where the stars are washed out.

Unless care is taken, Farmville and the surrounding communities may lose the night sky. A new library is rising. There is development underway south of Farmville on Commerce Road. A quarry has been proposed for the western edge of town. An immigration detention center is in the planning stages. If the light dome of Farmville spreads unchecked, the stars will literally lose their shine.

It does not have to be this way. New development can sprout, bringing jobs and economic growth, without sacrificing the natural darkness of night. It takes appropriate planning, however, and a commitment to use shielded and properly focused outdoor lights. When people use lights in this way, they help ensure the security of their neighbors on the ground by casting illumination where it is needed without creating blinding glare and wasting energy to light up the sky.

Judicious use of outdoor lighting is safer and healthier—for people and for the environment. Recently, the American Medical Association, noting that roadway safety is enhanced when glare is reduced, passed a resolution advocating the reduction of light pollution. Researchers have linked light at night to sleep-cycle disruptions, and those who study the environment claim that it interferes with bird migrations, bat populations, turtles, and a host of activities among nocturnal animals and insects.

People who want to learn more about different types and uses of outdoor lighting can contact the International Dark-Sky Association by phone at 520-293-3198 or through their website at http://www.darksky.org. The Virginia section of the International Dark-Sky Association also hosts a website at http://www.darkvirginiasky.org. It includes a night-time satellite map of the state with county lines superimposed. The lights of Farmville, unfortunately, are easily identified.

I admit that I'm a new kid in town, and I have a lot to learn about the community's dynamics and the people who influence policy. But, I'd like to believe that an interest exists in promoting health and safety while saving energy, money, and the environment. And, I'd like to believe that I'm not alone in thinking that the wonder-filled natural resource in the sky overhead at night is too precious to be abandoned.

A DIFFERENT KIND OF HISTORY
May 2010

One of the things I've learned to appreciate in Farmville is the history that enriches the area. Many famous names and events that star in history books—like Patrick Henry, Robert E. Lee, and the civil rights movement—have local connections.

But there's another kind of history, replete with its own stars, that nightly shines above us. Because light has to travel through space to reach our spot in the universe, viewing distant astronomical objects is like looking back in history. We see the objects as they were decades, centuries, and even millennia ago.

Would you like to see them for yourself? One resource for doing so is your nearest astronomy club. The Night Sky Network, a project of NASA's Jet Propulsion Laboratory, offers a tool that can help you find groups across the United States (visit https://nightsky.jpl.nasa.gov). Astronomy clubs often host star parties where you can peer through assortments of telescopes and binoculars. If you've never looked at the night sky with anything other than your unaided eye, you'll be amazed at what a simple pair of binoculars can show. For astronomical observing, choose a pair with a lens diameter of at least a 35 mm.

If you're outside after dark in May, two stars that will be in the sky are the pair Castor and Pollux, the famous twins of the constellation Gemini. To arrive for viewing in 2010 when this text was originally written, the light from Pollux had been traveling since 1976. The light from Castor had been on its way a little longer, since 1965—that's just one year after Prince Edward County reopened its schools following the Supreme Court's *Griffin v. County School Board* decision.

For people seeking a star with a Civil War connection, I recommended checking out Psi Ursa Major. The constellation Ursa Major is better known as the "Big Bear," and Psi Ursa Major is in its back leg. Light arriving in 2010 from Psi Ursa Major began its journey in 1863—the same year General Lee led 75,000 troops into Pennsylvania.

Ursa Major is also home of the star pattern commonly known as the Big Dipper. Two of the stars in the Big Dipper always point to Polaris, the North Star. At a distance of 430 light years, the starlight we saw from Polaris in 2010 was from 1580—that's the birth year of Captain John Smith, who is best remembered for his role in helping establish the Jamestown colony.

For a star with a connection closer to Farmville, ask someone to show you Spica, the brightest star in the constellation Virgo. Viewing it in 2010 revealed the star as it was in 1760—the year the young man Patrick Henry decided to become a lawyer.

For something a bit older, you may want to check out a faint, fuzzy patch high overhead in the constellation Cancer. This is the Beehive cluster—a grouping of stars resembling a swarm of bees. The light from this cluster started its journey to earth around 1460. At the time, Christopher Columbus was a lad of nine.

Deneb, a star in the constellation Cygnus, rises in the east during the late evening in May. Scientists estimate that it is one of the most intrinsically bright stars in the Milky Way galaxy. Although it is among the top 20 brightest stars in Earth's night sky, it is located more than 1,400 light years away (and some astronomers suggest it may even be more distant). Light from Deneb may have started its journey to Earth around the same time Muhammad, founder of the Islamic faith, reported having first received an angelic vision.

In addition to these far away objects, some nearer celestial neighbors also grace our night skies. Because they are closer to Earth, their movement is more apparent and the time of year during which they can be seen changes. The moon, which cycles through its phases every 29 days, is located at a distance of only about 1.2 seconds when measured according to the speed of light. Distances to other planets within our solar system can be measured in "light minutes" or "light hours" (as opposed to the "light years" that mark the distances to other stars).

The number of light minutes or hours as measured from Earth constantly changes, however, because the planets orbit the sun at different speeds. Sometimes Earth and another planet are on the same side of the sun, but at other times they are farther apart, located on opposite sides of the solar system. To give you an approximate sense of the scale of the solar system, here's a list of the planets and their average distance from the sun in light travel times: Mercury (3.2 minutes), Venus (6.0 minutes), Earth (8.3 minutes), Mars (12.5 minutes), Jupiter (43.2 minutes), Saturn (which is the most distant object in the solar system that can be seen by the unaided eye, 1.3 hours), Uranus (2.7 hours), and Neptune (4.2 hours). And, because I know many of you believe it should still be included in a roster of planets: Pluto (about 5.5 hours).

Whether you're looking at light from a few moments ago or from centuries ago, I hope you'll enjoy its beauty and the role the stars have played across many cultures throughout human history.

ONCE IN A BLUE MOON
August 2012

What is it that you do only once in a blue moon? Is it an indulgence? Something decadent like enjoying a whole bar of dark chocolate? Or is it pampering someone else? Perhaps taking someone a bouquet of flowers? Maybe it's a duty you put off until guilt drives you to action.

Whatever it is, you'll likely get your chance soon—at least within the next few years.

Although some people use the phrase "once in a blue moon" to refer vaguely to something that seldom happens, a blue moon actually arrives with some regularity. It doesn't occur frequently enough to be commonplace, but it does happen often enough to avoid being distant and remote.

According to contemporary folklore, a blue moon is the second full moon in a month. Full moons happen about every 29 days. Most of the time, there's one full moon every month. But occasionally one falls close enough to the beginning of the month that a second can occur near its end. By this definition, "once in a blue moon" usually happens once every two or three years.

February, which typically has only 28 days, sometimes has no full moon at all. When this happens, the January before and March after will both have blue moons. The next year with a doubling of blue moons in this fashion will be 2018.

Some folk fuss about technicalities and claim that the modern definition of a blue moon is based on a misunderstanding of a convoluted reckoning system that named the third full moon in a season that had four full moons as a blue moon without regard for the calendar month in which it occurred. *Farmers' Almanac* (http://www.farmersalmanac.com) explains that this seasonal rule was used by the *Maine Farmers' Almanac*, which was published in the early 1900s (and not related to the current *Farmers' Almanac*). This method of calculation doesn't make blue moons occur with any more or less frequency. They're just harder to calculate, and sometimes the seasonal rule causes the blue moon designation to override other traditional moon names. No wonder the simpler definition achieved greater popularity.

In the U.S., the tradition of naming full moons extends back to Native Americans. The moon names varied by region and among tribes, but according to *Farmers' Almanac*, these are among the most common:

January: Wolf Moon

February: Snow Moon

March: Worm Moon

April: Pink Moon

May: Flower Moon

June: Strawberry Moon

July: Thunder Moon

August: Sturgeon Moon

September: Harvest Moon (or Corn Moon)

October: Hunter's Moon (or Harvest Moon)

November: Beaver Moon

December: Cold Moon

The best known is probably the Harvest Moon. *Farmers' Almanac* explains that the Harvest Moon is the full moon that occurs closest to the autumnal equinox. Two years out of every three, it falls in September. When the Harvest Moon falls in October, the September Moon is called the Corn Moon.

But why are extra full moons called blue? Theories abound, and facts are scarce. My favorite supposition is based on an explanation offered by Infoplease (http://www.infoplease.com). They quote an old proverb suggesting that the moon turning blue is something absurd, something that is not likely to ever occur. In our modern use of the language we might convey the same meaning by suggesting that something will happen when someplace really hot freezes over.

As the English language changed through the centuries, the meaning associated with the moon turning blue drifted. Instead of implying "not likely," it came to mean "rarely." *The Oxford English Dictionary* records that the phrase was used in this way in the early 1800s. The modern definition as the second full moon in a month seems to have first made its appearance in an article published in 1946 in *Sky and Telescope* magazine.

But irrespective of why the moon is called blue or when it became enshrined in our calendars, you can be certain one is coming—at least within a few years. Based on the monthly definition, blue moons that have occurred since I began writing this column occurred on December 31, 2009, August 31, 2012, July 31, 2015, and May 21, 2016. As of this update, the next will be January 31, 2018. Those of you who prefer the seasonal definition, will have to wait until May 18, 2019.

HOPE REWARDED
November 2014

Several weeks ago I got up in the predawn darkness. Voluntarily. I wanted to see the lunar eclipse.

A lunar eclipse occurs when the sun, earth, and moon are aligned in a manner that causes the moon to pass through the earth's shadow. It can happen only when the moon is full, but an eclipse doesn't happen every month. Usually when the full moon slips behind the earth, it passes either above or below the shadow. Sometimes it enters partway into the shadow creating a partial lunar eclipse. Partial eclipses are fairly common, often a couple per year. Total eclipses are more infrequent, although they often occur in clusters. The one I got up to see was part of such a cluster. The total lunar eclipse of October 2014 was the second to occur in 2014. The cluster included one more visible in Farmville on September 28, 2015 (another on April 4, 2015 was only party visible here). As of this update, we're in a lull until the next one, which will occur in 2018.

Just because a lunar eclipse occurs, however, is no guarantee that it can actually be seen. Although lunar eclipses are more widely visible than their more elusive solar counterparts, you still have to be in the right place at the right time. And, the weather has to cooperate. For those of us in Farmville, the eclipse of April 2014 was obscured by clouds and rain.

The most recent eclipse was also nearly washed out. A shower passed through about an hour before its beginning. When I got up, clouds covered a significant patch of sky. Trees were still dripping. From my window, I couldn't tell if the moon would be visible or not. With a strong dose of optimism, I got dressed and walked to a spot where my view of the western sky was unobstructed by the landscape.

A brightly shining, fully round moon rewarded my hope. It wore a thin veil of cloud wisps, and then those clouds passed on. Larger portions of the sky opened up, and stars shone through. I noticed then that the moon didn't look quite full. The earth's shadow encroached upon one edge, and during the course of the next hour or so, its darkness seeped across the moon's face.

Normally, the moon looks white as it reflects the full spectrum of sunlight. A fully eclipsed moon takes on an orange glow because it reflects only sunbeams that have been bent by the earth's atmosphere. The moon's transformation bestowed an ethereal, enchanted ambiance to the approaching dawn. From our vantage point here in south-central Virginia, the moon remained in an eclipsed state until it set. It returned to the sky the next night as if nothing out of the ordinary had happened.

Although eclipses arrive in a predictable fashion (NASA's official eclipse website can be found online at http://eclipse.gsfc.nasa.gov/eclipse.html), their schedules are just a starting point. Each individual eclipse has its own personality. Atmospheric conditions on earth during its exact moments govern how deeply red or orange the moon appears. Clouds can blot out an entire event, but clouds can also enhance and add character to the occasion. The flare of a shooting star can bring unexpected drama. Sharing the encounter with a friend adds a special kind of fun. When eclipses occur in winter, shivering in the dark with numbed toes can make the experience uncomfortable.

Eclipses remind me of life. No matter how carefully I plan, no matter how far in advance I know something will happen, moment-by-moment surprises crop up, and even routine events can include unpredictable elements. I can plan and prepare dinner, but I don't know when a phone call—whether from an old friend or an anonymous sales person—will interrupt it. I can attend a weekly Bible study, but I can't predict when a new insight will present itself. I can even plan next year's vacation, but the wonders and disappointments that await will all take me by surprise. As I go through each day, just like when I watch an eclipse, I need to be awake to possibilities and let hope guide me to the best view.

STARRY, STARRY NIGHT ... OR NOT
July 2011

A surprisingly large number of you attended the Night Walk at High Bridge Trail State Park in June 2011. The event, hosted in celebration of Virginia State Parks' 75th anniversary, started at the train station and progressed to Buffalo Creek. Bob Flippen, the park's AmeriCorps volunteer at the time and a limitless fount of historical knowledge, pointed out sites along the way and talked about how Farmville's story is interwoven with the stories of our nation and even the world beyond.

My husband, Bruce, and I also played a role. We were supposed to point out the highlights in the night sky, making a connection between us and the entire universe. That was the plan anyway. The clouds had a different idea. As a result, the sky was not filled with twinkling beacons of distant light. In fact, for most of the evening, finding the full moon was a challenge.

Nevertheless, during one twenty-minute interval the clouds parted slightly. The gap afforded a glimpse of the International Space Station as it passed overhead, fourteen stars (yes, I counted all of them), and one planet—Saturn. After the clouds closed in again, Bruce explained several models for helping the human mind grasp the vast distances of space. For example, if the entire distance between the earth and sun (about 93,000,000 miles) were represented by just one inch, on the same scale the closest star to our sun would be more than four miles away.

At the end of the program and during the days that followed, people asked me lots of questions. I'd like to answer some that have come up often:

"When will the International Space Station pass overhead again?" The ISS orbits the earth about once every 90 minutes, but its path and orientation need to be properly aligned for us to see it. My favorite way to find out when it will be visible is through a website called Heavens Above (http://www.heavens-above.com; the hyphen is an important part of the website address). You don't have to log in to access information, but if you choose to log in (which is free), you can set it to remember your location and local time. If you click on the ISS link, it will give you a ten-day list of all visible passes for your location. NASA also offers a service called Spot the Station (https://spotthestation.nasa.gov).

"Where can I get a map of the sky for a particular night?" One of the easiest places to get a basic map is also Heavens Above. Just click on the link that says "Whole Sky Chart" and enter the date and time you want. The chart will have north at the top, but east and west will appear to be reversed. This isn't a mistake. Hold the chart over your head with north to the north, and you'll see that the compass points are properly aligned to the sky when you look up at it.

"Can I see other planets?" Five planets in our solar system are visible to the unaided eye. Over time, they move around against the background of stars. During the night of our cloudy program, Saturn was the only one visible before midnight. Other planets that can be seen easily without optical aid—when they are in appropriate alignment—are Venus, Mars, and Jupiter. Mercury can be a bit harder to spot. Mercury makes only brief appearances at dawn and dusk when its relative position puts it off to one side of the sun or the other.

And, perhaps the number one question: ***"What kind of laser pointer is that?"*** It's a green laser. Unlike red lasers, which produce a point of light only when they strike a surface, a green laser also slightly scatters its light in the air. The resulting effect produces a straight green line that can stretch toward space, perfect for pointing out stars. I hope the next time I get to use it, there will be more than fourteen stars to see.

THE COMETS ARE COMING
March 2013

In early 2013, headlines focused attention on the sky. An asteroid whizzed past the earth at a distance close enough to pose a threat to some orbiting satellites. A meteor exploded over Russia. A fireball was photographed in California. Such things are common enough in geologic history, but on the scale of a human life span, they are rare events.

Sky watchers were also keeping close tabs on two recently discovered comets with the potential to become bright enough for casual observers to see: Comet PanSTARRS was discovered in June 2011 and named in honor of the telescope responsible for identifying it, the Panoramic Survey Telescope and Rapid Response System located on Mount Haleakala on the island of Maui in Hawaii. The second, Comet ISON, was discovered in September 2012 by the International Scientific Optical Network's telescope in Russia.

Astronomers use the term magnitude to describe an object's brightness. The magnitude scale uses lower numbers to refer to brighter objects and higher numbers to refer to dimmer objects. Some people find the inverse nature of the magnitude scale to be confusing, so it can be helpful to think of magnitudes like prizes: Winning first prize is better than winning third or fourth prize. In the same way, first magnitude is brighter than third or fourth magnitude.

Comet brightness predictions are notoriously tricky and often inaccurate. (At the end of this column's text, I'll provide some updated information about what happened to these two comets.) Magnitude predictions for Comet PanSTARRS, ranged from 0 to 3. Using the constellation Orion for comparison, its two brightest stars, Rigel (lower right) and Betelgeuse (upper left) have magnitudes of 0.2 and 0.5. Bellatrix, Orion's dimmer shoulder, has a magnitude of 1.6, and the three stars that form Orion's famous belt range in magnitude from 1.7 to 2.2. But, because a comet's light is spread over a larger area than the light from the single point of a star, a comet can appear dimmer than a star of the same magnitude.

Since its discovery, Comet PanSTARRS had been moving toward the sun and increasing in brightness. The best time to try to catch a glimpse of it from Farmville was just after sunset in mid-March 2013. To spot it, one needed an unobstructed view of the western horizon and a caution: To protect your eyes, do not look directly at the sun. And, if you're using binoculars or other optical aids before sunset, do not even look in the direction of the sun. Accidentally viewing the sun through these devices can cause permanent damage to your vision.

Comet PanSTARRS was at perihelion (its closest approach to the sun) on March 9 and 10, 2013. On the night of March 12, it appeared close to the thin crescent moon. As the days progressed, its distance from the sun gradually increased, and it rose a little higher in the twilight sky. Later in the month, its increasing distance from the sun caused it to become much fainter.

The year's second comet held the potential to be even more spectacular. Comet ISON made its closest approach to the sun on November 28, 2013. Some scientists believed its brightness could have potentially rivaled that of the full moon.

In March 2013, I co-hosted an event at High Bridge Trail State Park to help people learn more about comets and prepare for observing these cosmological treats.

Here's an update: Comet PanSTARRS made its appearance just as predicted. Finding it proved to be simple with a small telescope, but locating it with an unaided eye was more problematic. Because it was low in the western sky just after sunset, the comet's brightness had to compete with the lingering twilight. As the sky got dark, the comet set. Nevertheless, my husband and I enjoyed watching it for several days.

As anticipated, Comet ISON approached the inner solar system in late November 2013. Astronomers held their collective breaths as it made a flyby of the sun on Thanksgiving Day. Had the comet survived this encounter, it may have gone on to present a spectacular display in Earth's skies. That's not what happened. The sun's gravitational effects pulled the comet apart, and the debris that remained was too small to be visible from an earth-based platform.

PLAN B
March 2014

My husband and I had the privilege of leading an astronomy event on March 1, 2014 at High Bridge Trail State Park. From the middle of High Bridge the sky is unobstructed from horizon to horizon. Plan A was to point out the constellation Orion and other sky patterns related to the Greco-Roman mythological accounts of his exploits. Then we were going to use a telescope and binoculars to look at some of the special treats that can be better viewed with optical aid. Among these is the Orion nebula, a region of active stellar formation where a delicate cloud-like wisp of gases reflect the light of nearby stars.

After months of planning, the day arrived. Cold and overcast. Then it cleared. Then it clouded up again. And then it cleared. And so it went until late afternoon. I bundled up in my quilted stadium coat, put on two pairs of thick socks, and securely fastened a hat over my ears. By sunset, we had hauled our equipment out onto the bridge so we could get it set up before darkness fell. Overhead, an unbroken cloud bank stretched in all directions. There was one thin ribbon of clear sky hovering over the western horizon. We watched it, hoping it would grow.

It did not. We saw Plan A waft away, vanishing among the clouds.

Fortunately, Plan B stepped up to take its place. As the earth turned, a vividly red setting sun emerged from below the clouds to cast a pink and orange glow over the Appomattox River valley. The treetops sparkled with captured light. Within minutes the orb of the sun sank and disappeared below the horizon. As it did, its rays cast themselves up onto the underside of the clouds. Rosy coloration seeped across the sky and mingled with purple that had previously been grey. Then the tiny band of clear sky along the horizon began to glow a brilliant yellow. The sun, our solar system's very own star, was putting on its own show.

After several minutes, the sunset's brilliance faded, and other features of the evening stepped up to be enjoyed. While we listened, a single frog began a song announcing that—despite the cold of the day—spring was actually just around the corner. The light continued to fade. More frogs joined in the chorus. A pair of ducks flew beneath the bridge apparently heading home for the night. The distant sound of the rushing river reminded us that winter was washing away.

The night deepened and tiny transitory holes opened in the clouds. We played a game of "Name that Star!" Stars are typically identified by noting their positions and appearance within larger patterns. Recognizing them when only one at a time could be seen was like trying to "Name that Tune" in just one note. Eventually, we found a spot where the planet Jupiter was playing a celestial game of hide and seek. It peeked through the clouds for a few seconds and disappeared. It repeated the performance often enough that we were eventually able to get the telescope fixed on it. That enabled us to catch glimpses of the bands that famously mark its surface and to see the four Jovian moons that were first identified by Galileo.

The big guy, Orion, didn't make an appearance at all. After the event was over and everything was packed away, he peered out, but by then it was too late to share.

The constellation Orion has been in the sky throughout the winter. With spring approaching, he's making his way toward the western horizon, setting four minutes earlier every day. By late May, he'll be gone, and other constellations will watch over our summer nights.

If you want to discover the stars and the stories missed while we were enjoying an evening of Plan B, I invite you to go online and read my blog about Orion the Hunter. You can find it in *Pier Perspectives* http://pierpress.com/pierperspectives/2014/2/19/orion-the-hunter/. The blog also includes instructions for downloading a sky map to help you identify the constellations. Then, find a convenient night, step outside, and enjoy whatever presents itself.

FINDING NORTH
April 2015

When I conduct sky tours in conjunction with astronomy programs offered at High Bridge Trail State Park, the number one question people ask is this: "Where's the Big Dipper?" The next thing they ask is, "How does it guide the way north?"

Springtime provides a wonderful opportunity to answer both questions. Finding the Big Dipper involves knowing where to look and what orientation to expect.

This time of year, in the darkness that follows sunset, the Big Dipper hangs in the northeastern sky. If you're not sure where northeast is, try this trick: Find a convenient landmark near the location where the sun slips below the horizon, and remember the spot. When it's dark enough for the stars to be visible, go outside, stand tall, and hold your arms straight out at your sides. Turn your whole body so that your left arm points to where the sun set. Then, turn your head just a little to the right. You'll be gazing in the general direction of northeast.

Spotting the Big Dipper's pattern can still be challenging if you don't know how big "Big" is or what angle to expect. The Big Dipper's apparent size is fairly easy to estimate. If you hold your hand out at arms' length and extend your little finger and thumb as far as you can stretch them, they will delineate a piece of sky nearly as long as the Big Dipper (maybe even as long if you have flexible fingers).

The Big Dipper's orientation depends on the season and the hour. Last month (March) after sunset, the Big Dipper would have appeared to be standing almost straight up on its handle. Because the Earth's location changes as it orbits around the sun, every day the stars appear to reach the same position in the sky four minutes earlier. As a result, this month during the first few hours of darkness, the Big Dipper will appear higher and its bowl will seem angled toward the earth. As midnight approaches, the Big Dipper will arch high overhead. Then, in the early morning hours, it will descend bowl-side-down in the northwest. Although you won't be able to observe it in the daytime, if you could, you would see that the Big Dipper's motion makes a circle every twenty-four hours. To be more precise, the Earth (our observing platform) makes a complete revolution on its axis every day, and that motion makes it seem like the stars are circling around a point in space.

That point, known as the celestial North Pole, rests directly above the Earth's North Pole. The spot is currently occupied by a very special star, the North Star, which is also called Polaris. Because the Earth's axis of rotation wobbles slowly over millennia, Polaris hasn't always been in this convenient location, and in the distant future it will yield its seat of honor to other stars. Nevertheless, for the present (measured in human lifespans), Polaris appears stationary. Furthermore, it is visible throughout the entire northern hemisphere. In the days before GPS, these special attributes made Polaris an important object for navigation.

Finding the middle of a huge celestial circle may seem challenging, but two of the stars in the Big Dipper clearly point the way. Those two stars are called the "Pointer Stars." They are at the end of the Big Dipper's bowl on the side opposite its handle. If you draw a line from the star at the bottom of the bowl, through the one at the top of the bowl and extend that line about four times the distance, you'll come to Polaris. Irrespective of the Big Dipper's position during the night or during the year, these two stars always point toward Polaris.

If you're interested in learning more or trying your hand at celestial navigation, read "Making a Simple Astrolabe" from *Pier Perspectives* http://pierpress.com/pierperspectives/2015/4/18/making-a-simple-astrolabe.

A BLOOD-RED SUPER HARVEST MOON
September 2015

The moon over Farmville put on quite a show in September 2015. During the early days of the month, the moon's opening act featured its waning (diminishing) phases, and the moon rose later on successive nights. People who got up before dawn were treated to a slender crescent that slipped between Venus and Mars about an hour before sunrise on September 10. Then the curtain closed briefly, and the new moon was hidden from view on September 13.

The curtain rose for the moon's next act on September 14, when a thin sliver appeared low in the western sky just after sunset. The width of this crescent increased as the next nights passed. This stage is known as waxing (think of how a candle can be made thicker by dipping it in warm wax). The moon's position also changed, moving eastward against the starry background and traversing about 13 degrees of sky every day.

The moon reached first quarter during the morning hours of September 21, just two days before the autumnal equinox (which marks the beginning of fall). After that, the moon continued growing through a phase known as "waxing gibbous" until it reached full on the evening of Sunday, September 27.

That particular full moon promised to be a spectacular, grand finale for the month-long show.

In American folklore, the full moon closest to the autumnal equinox is called the Harvest Moon. According to tradition, the full moon's light at this time of year extends the hours during which farmers can bring in their crops.

Although that might be sufficient grounds for celebration, the Harvest Moon had additional marvels in store. It was also a "super" moon. The moon's slightly elliptical orbit brings it closer to the earth at some points (as close as 225,000 miles) and takes it farther away at others (a distance of more than 250,000 miles). The farthest point is called the "apogee," and the closest point is called the "perigee." According to NASA, the apparent total area of a full moon at perigee is fourteen percent bigger than at apogee. It is also thirty percent brighter. Those numbers may sound impressive, but in reality the difference isn't enough for casual observers to notice. Still, it's fun to know when a Harvest Moon will present our nearest celestial neighbor at its closest, largest, and brightest "super" state.

But that's not all. That Harvest moon had one additional treat in store for observers. A total lunar eclipse occurred during the late evening hours of September 27. The moon entered the earth's umbra (the deepest part of its shadow) at about 9:06 p.m. Eastern Daylight Time. Over the course of the next hour, the earth's shadow crept across the lunar face. After the moon passed fully into the umbra, it took on a coppery orange hue. This reddish coloration is responsible for giving rise to the popular term "blood moon." The moon remained in this fully eclipsed state for an hour and twelve minutes. The entire event, from the moon's first encounter with the umbra until it completely exited the dark shadow, took three hours and twenty minutes. If you missed it, the next total lunar eclipse won't occur until January 31, 2018, and it will be only partially visible from Farmville.

NASA's Eclipse Website at http://eclipse.gsfc.nasa.gov/eclipse.html can help you plan for upcoming solar and lunar eclipses.

Summers & Vacations

IT'S GOOD TO BE BACK HOME AGAIN
June 2012

I love to travel, to pack my bags and head for destinations near and far. Discoveries and wonder wait around every corner. There are people to visit and sights to see. Surprises can pop up almost anywhere. I have seen the northern lights, and I have seen the Southern Cross.

On a recent visit to Staunton, Virginia, I saw a Shakespearean play performed with such tangible emotion, I forgot I was listening to lines written 400 years ago. I felt as if the events were unfolding right before my eyes. I experienced the people's griefs and joys. Their passions touched my heart.

On a different trip earlier in the year, I stood on the shore of Lake Michigan. I watched a whipping wind dash six-foot waves against a pier, and I forgot the present. My mind was transported back through centuries, and I saw countless voyages made by desperate people across many treacherous waters. Their courage humbled me.

But lately I've been beckoned here and there with more frequency than is comfortable, and I'm discovering the simple joys of coming home.

If I've been south, I come home by driving up Route 15 from North Carolina. I feel the first thrill of homecoming when I cross the Virginia state line. There's a small bump in the pavement that provides a physical lurch to intensify the emotion of the moment. The eagerness to be home deepens when I cross Buggs Island Lake. A few miles later,

Route 15 merges onto Route 360. The multilane highway with its faster speed limits helps build momentum as my destination draws near. I pass Keysville, and I know it won't be much farther. Route 15 disentangles itself from Route 360, and I soon see the sign for Hampden-Sydney College. Before long, I hear the familiar crunch of the gravel on my street. The overarching trees extend their branches in a welcome. My driveway awaits, and my front porch reaches toward the car to greet me.

From points north, getting off I-64 in Charlottesville is like exiting life's rat race and settling into the comfort of more familiar things. Steeply undulating fields gradually become gentler, and then the road dips into Scottsville. Crossing to the south side of the James River returns me to Southside Virginia, and I know the journey is nearly done. I pick up Route 15 south in Dilwyn. Making that turn signifies the transition from being away to being back. I cross Route 60. Sprouse's Corner. Curdsville. Sheppards. Finally the Appomattox River. And then, my corner.

When I come home from visiting family in Michigan, the trip spans several states. I cross the Virginia line in the mountains fourteen miles west of Covington. There's a big welcome sign, and I smile and take it personally. "I'm back!" I tell the sign. Theoretically, I know I could get home more quickly by taking the winding road across the mountain that looms over Buena Vista, but I usually opt for the milder terrain of the Shenandoah Valley. That enables me to pick up Route 460 just north of Roanoke. Then it's Bedford. Lynchburg. Appomattox. By the time I reach Prospect, I glimpse parts of High Bridge Trail where I have walked and ridden my bike. That surely qualifies as home.

The car comes to a rest at the end of the driveway. I stretch my stiff legs. Then I'm at ease in a familiar kitchen. I don't need a map to find the grocery store. My favorite chair is waiting just where I left it, and my calendar promises the comfortable rhythm of ordinary days to come.

I'm not sure when family, business, or even wanderlust will call me away again, but for the time being, I plan to sit on the porch. I'm going to put my feet up and watch the clouds. I'm going to listen to familiar birds and eat in restaurants where the waiter already knows what I want.

Yet, even here, even back home, discoveries and wonder wait around every corner. There are people to visit and sights to see. Surprises can pop up almost anywhere.

SEEING STARS
July 2012

On a recent Saturday afternoon, I saw an unfamiliar swirl of stars. Yes, that's right. I said "afternoon." Let me explain.

Long before my husband and I moved to Farmville, someone built the house we ultimately bought. They added a few special touches. One of my favorites is the breakfast bar that divides the kitchen from the dining room. Its top is a nearly black granite with large crystalline splotches of a brown that strays into the red part of the spectrum. There are also random thin streaks of white, and if I look closely I can see sparkles and hints of almost every other color in the rainbow. During a visit, one of my children discovered that some parts of it will even attract a magnet.

I don't often eat breakfast at the breakfast bar, at least during the summer. My favorite table for that activity is out on the back porch. But, I do use the breakfast bar frequently. Mail accumulates in front of my barstool, often in a wilting stack of magazines and catalogs that wait patiently for me to find a few minutes to sit down and peruse their pages.

So that brings us to the fateful Saturday. Earlier in the day, I had been outside. I don't remember exactly what I had been doing. I came in, poured myself a big glass of ice water, sat down, and started reading. It wasn't long before I kicked off my shoes and wriggled my toes. When I finished my water, I wandered off barefoot.

I suppose it was all the years I spent mothering—all the times I had called to one child or another to come back and pick up his or her shoes—that made me do it. I saw those shoes on the floor beside my stool. I intended to grab them and put them away.

In my haste, my body misjudged the lip of the countertop, and I smacked the back of my rising head directly against the granite. Like I said, I saw an unfamiliar swirl of stars. I think I heard bells, too.

My husband was standing in the kitchen. He may have started to ask, "What on earth are you doing?" but he only got as far as "Wha...?" before his emergency response instincts took over. "Sit down," he directed. "I'll get the ice."

I wobbled and obeyed.

Normally I enjoy seeing stars, but I usually opt for more familiar patterns and less painful opportunities. For example, there's the free, outdoor film series "Stars Under the Stars." Last month, in the movie *Pillow Talk*, two big name stars—Doris Day and Rock Hudson—fell in love while twinkling stars —including Spica and Antares—watched from above. The event is held at the Crute Stage in downtown Farmville. People bring blankets and lawn chairs, mingle with neighbors, and enjoy popcorn and candy. It's sort of like going to a drive-in without having to worry about bringing the car or finding a speaker that works. Other stars on display that summer included Gary Cooper and Grace Kelly (*High Noon*, Friday, July 13) and Julie Andrews and Dick Van Dyke (*Mary Poppins*, Friday, August 10). If you missed those stars, there's more to come every summer in Farmville. "Stars Under the Stars" gets underway at dusk on the second Friday of the month, at about 8:30 p.m. (rain dates are the following evenings).

More stars of the twinkling variety also shine during the summer nights. Three of the brightest are Vega, Deneb, and Altair. Together they form a pattern called the Summer Triangle. The Summer Triangle rises in the east after sunset and watches over us through the fall. On dark nights, the fainter Milky Way boils out of the spout of a star pattern that looks just like a teapot.

If you'd like a guided tour of the night sky, check the schedule at High Bridge Trail State Park (http://www.dcr.virginia.gov/state-parks/high-bridge-trail) to find out when the next astronomy event is planned. If the night is clear, you'll see stars from horizon to horizon—and it won't hurt a bit.

IN A HURRY
April 2013

My grandmother used to say, "The hurried-er I go the behind-er I get." In her opinion, rushing seldom worked to speed up results and quite often had the opposite effect. It's a lesson I never learned.

My life has often seemed to be characterized by dashing off here and there—finishing one thing and not quite catching my breath before the next was upon me. The habit became entrenched during the years I spent as a working mother with three children at home. I prided myself on the efficient use of every minute, and I experienced the thrill of victory when a day's pieces assembled into a precise order.

Upon moving to Farmville, however, I learned that some folks enjoy the process of walking through their days at a different pace. I first noticed this at the grocery store when the cashier would carry on complete conversations with everyone: How's your mother doing? You don't say? Bless her heart! You planning on making strawberry jam again this year? And, I'd think: Those strawberries are going to rot before any of us get out of this store.

Narrow roads were another spot frequented by people who preferred life in a slower lane. I'd come up behind two idling cars sitting side by side while drivers discussed the weather, the price of gas, or how "Those Ravens" were doing.

I adapted to these kinds of interruptions in my schedule, and for the most part, I think I managed to remain polite. I didn't tap my foot impatiently, sigh loudly, or drum my fingers. I didn't honk. But I didn't learn to idle. Instead, I bought a new phone that lets me use unfilled minutes to check my e-mail, scan the headlines, or even look up what "Those Ravens" are (a professional football team).

The fact that I was still living under the tyranny of needing to tuck something into every moment became evident one recent evening. I was making dinner. The table was set. The chicken in the oven needed 15 more minutes. According to its box, the rice on the stove needed 25. The vegetables slated for the microwave were only going to take six minutes, so they were still in the freezer.

I had two choices. I could relax until dinner reached a stage that required me to do something. Or, I could avoid wasting those minutes by taking care of some work that was sitting on my desk. Actually, I never considered that I had choices. I just set the alarm on my phone to alert me in 15 minutes, and I sprinted down the hall to my office. It seemed only a brief moment before my phone was buzzing and I took off again, back to the kitchen.

The oven timer was beeping, but my rice was sizzling and cracking. I pulled it off the stovetop burner as a smoke cloud rolled through three rooms. My husband helped me open some doors to air the place out, and I started scraping the blackened pan. I hadn't gotten far when a wind gust, knocked over a vase of flowers—pouring smelly water on a pile of unread mail.

I abandoned the burned pan, grabbed a towel, and started wiping. I dried each envelope and separated the pieces of soggy mail. Then I turned my attention to the puddle on the floor and tossed the towels into the washer.

Oh, yes, the oven was still beeping. I removed the now over-done chicken and set it on a trivet. The vegetables! They were still in the freezer. I popped them into the microwave. By the time they were done, I had to reheat the chicken.

Using those 15 minutes efficiently ultimately cost me half an hour—not counting the time required to finish cleaning the burned pan, re-sort the mail, and do the extra laundry. I finally recognized my grandmother's wisdom: The hurried-er I go, the behind-er I get.

So if you happen see me and it looks like I'm just poking along, please be patient. This is my new method of hurrying.

I'D RATHER BE
July 2013

I had the radio playing in my office the other day, and an old song sung by John Denver caught my ear: "I Guess He'd Rather Be in Colorado." My daughter lives in Colorado, so every time I hear that state's name it tugs on one of my heart strings. While I don't share her affection for the mountains and the snow, I understand that many people do. John Denver, who was born Henry John Deutschendorf, even took his professional name in honor of Colorado's capital city. This particular song examines the plight and longing of a man whose current view of the world comes to him through an office window and whose canyons are now the sidewalks and subways of New York.

As I listened to the song, I wished that the person it described could have traded places with Neil Diamond, who also often sang about feeling misplaced. Diamond's songs, however, seem to indicate he'd rather be in New York. "Brooklyn Roads" recalls his boyhood. "I Am I Said" describes living on the west coast and mourning the loss of his sense of community back east, and "Beautiful Noise" overflows with affection for the urban sounds of traffic, crowds, and commerce.

I thought about all the other places people would rather be and the things they'd rather be doing. One popular theme in bumper stickers and refrigerator magnets is "I'd Rather Be..." For one of my sons, he'd rather be flying. He has explained to me the joy of being in the sky, untethered. For me, flying is just a means of getting from point A to point B, but for him the sky means freedom, serenity, and limitless beauty.

There are many other slogans about places people would rather be and things they'd rather be doing: I'd Rather Be Camping, Fishing, Dancing, Shopping, Golfing, In Paris, At The Theater... The list is endless. It seems that most of us, if we had a choice, would rather be someplace else doing something different. I don't think I've ever seen a bumper sticker or T-shirt that said "I'm Content Right Here" or "I Just Love Working."

So I stopped to wonder where I would rather be and what I would rather be doing.

When I lived in Michigan, the question was easier to answer, especially in the winter. I would sit by my window, sip hot coffee, and look out over a bleak and frozen landscape. My thoughts were predictable: I'd rather be someplace warmer. I'd rather go for a walk in the sunshine. I'd rather listen to songbirds. Here in Farmville, I have that entire list of preferred things, and there isn't any place on earth I'd rather live.

But, I must admit, there are still times when a longing for something else sneaks up on me. Recently, my husband had to take me to the beach for a couple days. I needed to hear the surf. I needed to walk in the sand. I needed to smell the salt spray. I didn't want to be there permanently, but for a couple days I wanted to be someplace where my eyes could focus on the horizon and where my computer didn't keep reminding me that I had work to do.

In truth, I enjoy my work. I'd miss it if I didn't have it. And, although I loved watching dolphins and listening to gulls, if we'd stayed overlong at the shore, I would have started to miss the fields, the cows, and the wind whispering in the leaves. After a while, my bumper sticker might have read "I'd Rather Be in Farmville."

Perhaps all the things we'd rather be doing are simply the ingredients that make us who we are. When the recipe of our lives becomes unbalanced we respond with nostalgia and dreams about the parts that have gone missing.

Wherever it is you long to be and whatever it is you long to be doing, I hope the weeks ahead bring you a chance to incorporate them into your life in a meaningful way. I wish you a summer filled to the brim with the people, places, and activities you love.

GOING DOWN?
August 2014

After a whirlwind summer that included eleven states and nearly six thousand miles, Farmville looks really good to me. One of the things I love about being home is that my daily routine doesn't involve elevators. Trips out of town, especially when they include cities, almost always require journeys in elevators.

Oh, sure, if you look hard enough you can find elevators in Farmville. In the Corner Building, for instance, if you wanted to, you could ride an elevator all the way up to the third floor. If you wanted to. And, if you live or work on the Longwood campus, you might ride in one on a regular basis. Fortunately, my own excursions onto the Longwood campus typically involve Jarman Auditorium, Molnar Hall, and the theater, all of which are, thankfully, at ground level.

I'm not phobic about elevators. Just experienced.

At one stage of my life, I was blissfully unaware of the fact that elevators didn't always function properly. Then one blustery day in Chicago my innocence came to an end.

I was staying in a hotel that had guest rooms high above commercial floors below. Just getting to the hotel's lobby required a six-floor trip in a nonstop elevator. Guest rooms were higher.

One afternoon, I pushed the down button to summon an elevator. When one arrived I stepped on, joining a young couple with a babe in arms. They were accompanied by a porter who was transporting their luggage on a cart. The doors closed. The elevator descended, and something went wrong. At first there was a bump, and then it felt like a free fall with an abrupt stop. And the elevator stayed put. The doors wouldn't open. We were stuck in the no-man's-land between the lobby and the street. My witty cell phone reported simply, "No service."

If you're going to get stuck in a hotel elevator, the best way to do it is with a level-headed hotel employee. The porter had a two-way radio that let him talk with his comrades at the street level. I hope never to be buried alive, but my supposition is that it feels somewhat akin to being stuck in an elevator. His radioed voice connection with the outside world was our only link to the land of the living.

After a while, we heard thumps and bangs and shouts. The elevator cage shook, and we trembled, not knowing how many floors remained between us and the bottom of the shaft. The radio told us that the fire department was on hand and that we'd be rescued soon. Just hang on and stay still.

Eventually, the elevator was lowered and the doors pried open. The firemen helped us climb out, and the ordeal was over.

I developed a habit of scrutinizing elevator inspection stickers (alas, not all states require them), not taking the first elevator car to arrive when I didn't like the looks of it, and preferring to walk up and down the stairs if the journey involved just a few floors. My peculiarities became the stuff of family jokes, and repeatedly I heard admonitions such as, "Come on. You've already been stuck in an elevator. What are the odds it could happen again?"

Odds indeed. It was last summer in Denver. On that ride, it was just me and a cosmetologist visiting from somewhere in Louisiana. The emergency call box inside the elevator connected us with someone who thought we were joking.

Now, based on my multiple experiences, I can make this report: If you're stuck in an elevator, it probably didn't really involve a free fall. It just felt that way to your knees when the cage stopped suddenly. If the emergency call phone inside connects with someone who thinks you're a prankster, just try again. They'll eventually summon the fire department. Rescues take about an hour. Firemen truly are heroes.

So now my family says, "What are the odds it could happen three times?" And I laugh with them, but then I head for the stairs. Happily, here in Farmville, it's never more than a few floors.

SUMMERTIME TASKS
July 2016

I use to-do lists to help me remember things. My list of routine household chores (make the bed, cook dinner, do laundry) is short enough to remember, but I have to write down everything else. If I plan to go to a meeting or meet someone for lunch, I write it down. I keep my lengthy list of work-related items organized by deadlines. I have a separate list of projects that are on hold while I wait for input from someone else.

So, when summer arrived, it was only natural that I start a list of all the things I wanted to do. Plant some flowers. Wash the windows. Clean the baseboards. Paint the living room. The list kept growing, and summer started to feel like work.

That seemed contrary to the purpose and spirit of the season. So, I tossed that list and made a new one. I'd like to share it with you.

1. Watch clouds. One of summer's most essential sights has to be fluffy cumulus clouds drifting across the sky, transforming into all manner of creatures and structures as they go. I've already seen a lumpy goldfish, an alligator, a dog sitting up to beg, and a man with a pipe.

2. Blow soap bubbles. I haven't done this since the last wedding I attended. Instead of the traditional tossing of rice, the bride and groom were whisked on their way through a gauntlet of bubbles. I recently realized I don't need to wait to be invited to someone's nuptials to re-experience the mystical beauty of watching shimmering globes of iridescent colors float off into the beyond. This summer, I'm going to do it all by myself.

3. Listen to evening's arrival. At the edge of the woods, it's amazing how noisy a quiet evening can be. As the sun sets, all manner of insects and frogs pick up their instruments and begin to play. Chirrup, churr churr, kee-kee. As they reach a crescendo, a whippoorwill often joins in. Sometimes a distant coyote adds a lugubrious note of drama. I'm going to sit on my back porch and open my ears.

4. Enjoy the scent of rain. When rain hits the soil, especially if the ground has been dry, it causes spores to be released into the air. They carry a distinctive smell. Sometimes you can even catch a whiff of it in the wind ahead of a storm. When the forecast calls for showers, I'm going outside to breathe deeply.

5. Make homemade lemonade. I've got a new, easy recipe for sparkling lemonade. Put ice in a tall glass. Add seltzer water, lemon-lime flavor works best. Top off with concentrated lemon juice. Stir. Enjoy. I like it unsweetened, but I prefer my iced tea that way, too. If you're used to sweet tea, you may want to add a teaspoon or two of sugar. If I feel the need to multitask, I can enjoy my lemonade while I'm doing something else.

6. Feel the sunshine. John Denver once sang about sunshine on his shoulders, but I particularly enjoy it in my hair and on my face. I love the warmth of it and the sensation of energy seeping into my body. I'm going to stand in the sun and soak it in. After a while, a drop of perspiration is sure to start trickling down my back. Then, I'll head for the shade where I can experience the subtle shift to a cooler temperature and perhaps a gentle breeze.

7. Take an afternoon nap. Although any random Sunday would be a perfect time to schedule this chore, I think I should tend to it as soon as possible. If I like it as much as I anticipate, I may need to do it several times before summer melts into fall.

If I stick to this list, my original roster of tasks may remain undone when summer comes to an all-too-soon close. But that won't matter. The items on this list are the ones most important to me. They'll help ensure that I don't miss summer's most crucial essentials.

NOT THE END
June 2011

May 21, 2011 was nearly my last day on earth. And, no, I'm not talking about the heavenly judgement that had been forecast. Although I'm not a theologian, I do know that the premillennial point of view is just one interpretation among others. And, I also know that when Jesus spoke about his second coming, he said no one on earth—himself included—knew the day and hour. So, when a person who had previously guessed incorrectly decided to promote revised calculations, I ignored the prediction. I simply went about my business assuming that May 21st would be like any other day.

Not having anything particular on my agenda, I started that Saturday off by sleeping until the sun was well above the horizon. When its light filtered through the curtains and stirred me awake, I shuffled down the stairs. After a cup's worth of caffeine oozed into my bloodstream, I set about doing rather normal things. I made the bed. I checked my e-mail. It wasn't long before the day found me in the car, heading northeast along Back Hampton-Sydney Road. That's the narrow, curvy, shoulderless road that picks up where High Street leaves off.

I don't really care for the roller-coaster effect of trying to take the road faster than its curves allow, so I slow down and keep both hands on the wheel. I also keep my car positioned in the right-hand lane, and I do not cross the double yellow lines.

On my fateful Saturday morning, as I approached a sharp curve, another car came around it heading toward me. This car, however, followed the peculiar local habit of centering itself over the yellow lines.

Half of it was positioned in my lane. I braked abruptly. If I'd had more warning, I would have screamed.

But, I did not have warning. A collision that could have been as effective as the rapture in removing my soul from its earthly vessel seemed inevitable. Then, at the very last millisecond the oncoming car swerved into its own lane and sped away.

My day was unalterably changed. No longer was it a normal day. It was the day that could have been my last.

And, I'd been given a reprieve.

Once I stopped shaking, the sky appeared bluer. The clouds fluffier. The air smelled fresher, and the breeze carried the fragrance of honeysuckle and clover. My original plan had been to ride my bike along High Bridge Trail, and that's what I did. But instead of just peddling through the miles, I paid attention to the butterflies and slowed down to see the wildflowers. I was even blessed to catch a glimpse of a baby groundhog.

Later in the afternoon, I spent some time in quiet reflection in my back yard. I listened to the sharp trill of a Carolina wren and the chattering of chimney swifts and I wondered: What would I do differently if I knew it would really be my last day on earth?

The answer took me by surprise. Not much. Yes, I'd feel wretched knowing my family would endure a time of grief. And, I'd be sad about unaccomplished dreams. I'd be wistful about books I haven't yet read, projects that aren't started, and hopes and aspirations for things that may lie in the years ahead. But in terms of what would I actually do differently on a particular day, I couldn't think of a thing.

The truth emerged slowly. I actually felt satisfied and content. The title of my column is "Happy to Be Here," and I am. I don't feel ready to abandon all the wonders of God's creation and I certainly don't want to surrender the abundant joys of life to the vagaries of careless traffic, but I have a deep confidence that nothing in the world compares with what awaits at the end of this life's journey. I am in God's hands.

Only one thing is sure. Someday will be the last day of my life on earth. And when that day comes, whenever it comes, I hope it finds me still content and without regrets.

THE CHURCHES OF FARMVILLE
August 2011

People often ask if I've found a church home since moving to the area. The truth is I have been warmly welcomed at every church I've attended in Farmville, and I feel completely at home in many. At one point, I could tell you how many different churches I had visited, but two and a half years into my wanderings, I've lost count.

Farmville's churches include huge gatherings of several hundred people and cozy congregations of a dozen. Some feature old-fashioned pipe organs, some have modern worship bands with electric instruments and energetic drums, some have a quiet piano, and at least one doesn't use instruments at all. In some churches, the inspiring contributions of practiced choirs lifts my thoughts heavenward, and in others the music is simple enough that I can lift my own voice and join in.

The styles of the services vary as well. There are churches with rites and traditions that have been handed down for centuries. When I attend them, I feel a connection with earlier generations of faithful people. I am conscious of the symbolic and metaphoric components of the service, and they deepen my understanding of spiritual truths in a way that transcends what I can learn through mental effort alone. Other churches are less formal and even innovative. I enjoy their spontaneity and the awe-inspiring quiet joy that can permeate an entire congregation in a single moment. Each type of service offers a different version of reverence and meets the needs of different pieces of my emotional, intellectual, and spiritual being.

Farmville's churches also gather in diverse places. Some meet in solid, stone structures where flocks of the faithful have gathered under beautiful stained glass for more than a century. Some meet in new buildings with modern sound systems and comfortable seating arrangements. Still others gather in buildings that are used for other purposes during the regular work week, and each finds its own ways to make the space holy.

The church that meets at the local movie theater enjoys its role as an informal place for people who have experienced either too much or too little religion. They embrace the space available to them by passing a popcorn bucket instead of a more traditional collection plate. On the other hand, the church that meets at the Y, stands in sharp contrast to its allotted spot. I've been to the Y during the week, and I've worked hard and I've sweated. On Sunday mornings, however, the church that meets there uses very simple touches to transform a room into a serene, peacefully hallowed space. The transformation itself is miraculous.

While I enjoy the wide diversity of experiences that shape Farmville's faith communities, one of the things that impresses me the most is how much they share in common. Children find friends and grow into adults. Parents share the common task of raising children. College students far from home find mutual support and surrogate families. Lonely people find places where they can belong and where their talents are appreciated. Grandparents and great-grandparents pass along the faith they have demonstrated for a lifetime. People gather to celebrate on occasions of joy, offer comfort during times of distress, and provide support in the face of unspeakable sorrow or grief. And through all of these actions, even in the very smallest kindness, God is revealed, and I stand in awe watching.

Our entire region benefits because so many people dedicate themselves to establishing and nurturing specific individual congregations. Churches need dependable people to serve in ministry and governance roles. Without such dedication, there would be no local churches.

For myself, however, I believe I have a different role to play. When I stop by and join in a church's worship, I hope its congregation understands that it has connections beyond its own walls, that it has friends who stand with it, and that it is a vital part of a much bigger kingdom. I hope this brings encouragement.

So, if I haven't been to your church yet, please invite me. I'd love to come and worship with you.

BESIDE STILL WATERS
September 2012

Where do you go when life overwhelms you? When demands pile up and obligations seem to slip tentacles around your neck? When the frenetic pace of activities leaves you breathless and when looming deadlines nudge your blood pressure ever higher?

Where do you go when worries mount? When a previously secure job wavers or a parent's health falters? When it rains or when it doesn't?

Where do you go when emotions become tangled, and you're not sure whether you're worried or angry or just afraid? When you recognize your inability to help someone you love? When grief knocks on your door?

Gerry Goffin and Carole King wrote a song, "Up on the Roof," that was popular during the early 1960s. It proposed the rooftop as a refuge where the world below doesn't intrude. The lyrics suggest that rooftops can be peaceful havens of relative quiet that are physically and mentally distant from the rat race. Rooftops also have clearer air and are closer to the stars. Perhaps.

For myself, I can't imagine escaping anxiety by climbing onto a roof. The mere thought sets off twinges of latent acrophobia (fear of heights) mixed with a sprinkling of batophobia (fear of tall buildings) and a touch of barophobia (a fear of gravity). Unless the proposed rooftop sanctuary came with a sturdy fence system and ample safety margins, the possibility that gravity might reach up and drag me over the edge would overcome any other beneficial attributes of the location.

To find serenity, I need to have my feet on the ground. Just about any green space can be helpful, but when I need to soothe a mind filled with muddle, a shoreline suits me best. It doesn't have to be an ocean beach with pounding surf. Almost any patch of water will do.

Two of my favorite local spots are Wilck's Lake and Briary Creek Lake. Both provide various options for sitting or walking near the water's edge and letting my mental silt settle so my thoughts can clear.

Undulating swells and ripples lead to meditative stillness. A sprinkle of sunshine on the water quiets my mind, and I watch fluid points of light bob and sparkle. A nearly imperceptible breeze stirs the water, creating a darting ruffle for my eyes to chase. A stronger gust makes small wavelets that wink and blink. Daily hassles melt into their silver patina.

On windy days, whitecaps appear and I think about the calm that lies just below the surface. On quiet days, a fish jumps, and I remember that an amazing realm exists just beyond my sight.

In moments of mirror-like stillness, the reflection of shoreline trees creates a world turned upside down. "Yes!" I agree. Sometimes my world feels upside down. Then a wafting breath of wind blurs the image, and the inverted trees become a vague pattern of indistinct greens. The transformation reminds me of the difference between illusion and reality.

Underwater currents create differences in the water's surface texture, and I know that the things I hide within my heart create differences in the way I relate to others. A shadow from a passing cloud casts a spot of darkness that lingers for a moment and then drifts away. That's what spots of darkness do. They linger and then drift away. Even storms pass.

Twigs and leaves float, content to drift where the water takes them. I rebuke them. I insist that sometimes you need to paddle like mad. They nod on the waves, but they remind me that it's also sometimes okay to be satisfied with wherever the water goes.

I know I'm not alone in discovering that still waters are ideal for quiet reflection. Psalm 23, perhaps the most famous of the Psalms, begins "The Lord is my shepherd." It goes on to say, "He leads me beside still waters. He restores my soul."

That song about the rooftop: It builds to the moment of realizing there's room for two. But if you're like me and you'd rather have your feet on the ground, I invite you to the water's edge. There's room to share.

Colder Days & Warmer Hearts

FALLING IN LOVE WITH FALL

November 2009

People have their favorite seasons. For me, it has always been spring. After a cold, hard, dark winter, the world begins to awaken. Daylight lingers longer. Nature stirs. Plants revive. Life comes back to places it had seemingly abandoned.

But, last month, October stole my heart.

It began on the first, a Thursday. My son, who still lives in Michigan, called to say that he had to scrape ice off his windshield before leaving for work that morning. I told him about sitting on my back deck watching butterflies. I described the hummingbird that lingered longer than I thought it might. I mentioned that I couldn't see a cloud of breath when I exhaled no matter how hard I tried.

I have never before liked October. In my mind, the waning daylight and cold winds that strip branches bare represent defeat. Trees and flowers dying. Turtles and frogs hibernating. Chimney swifts abandoning me for their vacation homes. Signs that another year is staggering toward an untimely end. October has always snuck up on me, bringing with it a cloudy pall that would settle over my mood as it tucked the countryside in for a long—a very long—winter's nap.

This year, however, my shift of latitude helped the month woo me. October did bring a few days where temperatures dipped into the sweater range, but it didn't put an end to the bike rides I had enjoyed all summer. It didn't even keep me from having my morning coffee out on our back deck.

I know winter is still coming. Walks in the moonlight will be exchanged for a good book and warm blanket. I'll want my coffee hot instead of iced. But this year, the transition has been more gentle than what I've been accustomed to experiencing. I found comfort in the fuzzy warmth of sweatshirts. I was inspired to make soup.

Although the amount of daylight shortened, darkness failed to conquer. Instead, the gloom yielded to a different brightness, to the awakening colors as summer greens blossomed into gold, orange, and red. Even the stars helped hold the dark at bay as they twinkled so much brighter in the autumn evening air. And at regular intervals, the sun popped out with invitations to stroll through the woods or work in the yard. Instead of feeling confined, I felt the delicious ecstasy of a child permitted to stay up past bed time.

I admit that part of the new fun I discovered in October did have to do with the perverse joy of gloating. Telling someone stuck in different geography, "I'm so sorry you're having a gloomy, drizzly day. Only 38 degrees, you say? Well, we're having a cold day, too." Pause for dramatic effect. "It's only 50." What a difference those dozen degrees make.

But my new perspective has substance beyond this. For the first time, I felt a connection with the ingathering of autumn. As I watched squirrels tug acorns from the ends of branches and thought about farmers harvesting the fruits of their season of labor, I began to think about all the things—people and memories—I hold dear. I was struck with the notion that I needed to keep them close, to hold them in my heart for all the times to come. I finally grasped what it meant to be grateful for my many blessings, and I finally understood why Thanksgiving occurs in the fall.

Perhaps in years to come, my internal chronometer will adjust itself to the way seasons come and go at this latitude. I may even come to anticipate this tender season of summer's last embrace. But although I may come to expect and even look forward to October's glorious days, I hope I never take them for granted.

WORTH GETTING UP FOR
November 2010

Morning comes early in Farmville. I suppose that's because generations have needed to rise at dawn to feed cows and chickens or tend to harvests.

My husband fits right in. If you suggest meeting for breakfast at 7:00 a.m., he'll have eggs and pancakes. Or if you want to go fishing before the sun clears the horizon, his tackle box stands ready. He has always been among those people who wake up fully the moment their eyes pop open. His morning routine begins as if the starting gun at a race had been fired. In an instant, he's off at full stride.

Me? My mornings are more like trying to get the first bit of ketchup from a glass bottle. It takes some gentle shaking, followed by more persistent jostling, and finally jabbing or poking. When my first eyelid flutters, I simply settle back into sleep. It takes a significant amount of sunlight filtering through the curtains to cause my consciousness to rise to a vague awareness. At first, I merely note how comfortable the bed is, then I delight in the softness of the blanket and the luxury of the pillow. I take a deep breath, roll over, and retrieve whatever wispy fragments I can recall of abandoned dreams. Eventually, I stumble into the day. Twenty minutes after rising, I'll be capable of uttering a complete sentence. By thirty minutes, I can carry on a conversation. But not before.

It has always been this way for me. My mother used to scold me, using the frequently quoted adage: "The early bird gets the worm!" I'd reply, "Worms for breakfast? No thank you!"

To be sure, I've seen some marvelous sunrises. I recall one in particular where the last thin crescent of the waning moon hovered over the horizon, and another where Venus gleamed jewel-like in the darkness before surrendering its brilliance to the light of the new day's sun. Alas, I have enjoyed events such as these because I was still up, not because I got up.

So, when I first volunteered to work at FACES (Farmville Area Community Emergency Services), I was a little shaken, but not really surprised, when they suggested I show up at eight o'clock. "In the morning?" "Yes, in the morning." And on Saturday.

I typically volunteer once a month. On that precious day of the week when rolling over for a few extra stolen minutes of sleep is actually sanctioned, I set my alarm clock. I leave time for one, and only one, round of hitting the snooze button.

When I arrive at the FACES building, people are invariably lined up waiting for the doors to open. I don't know how long the first ones have been waiting. Sometimes they wait in cold, frosty morning air. Sometimes in the rain. And sometimes in record-setting blazing heat. They wait for hours as the line inches forward.

I am always surprised at the variety of people who come to receive a bag of groceries. Parents with small children in tow. Parents with adult children and even grandchildren who have moved back to their homes because of the hard economic times. Elderly people who can't afford both food and medicine. And people of all ages with various physical or mental disabilities. Some are recently out of work, and I recall one who was recently out of jail and eager to start a new life on a different path. Some come to sign up and can't write their names without assistance—a legacy of the era during which local schools were closed. The people in line represent diverse age groups and races, but they share a common need for the most basic stuff of life.

One recent Saturday morning, the volunteers at FACES—folk from a couple local churches, a group of students from Longwood University, and a few faithful regulars—handed out 853 bags of groceries. There were some sore backs and aching hands when it was all finished, but the atmosphere was jubilant. A celebration that such a tremendous need had been met. Yes, indeed, I was glad I had gotten up for it.

APPLESAUCE!
November 2012

Our Thanksgiving table will have a special addition this year. Applesauce.

I know what you're thinking: What's so special about applesauce? Aren't you supposed to have cranberry sauce for Thanksgiving?

Well, yes, cranberries will have a role on our table. My mother-in-law used to make a wonderful cranberry jelly that jiggled in all the right places and was topped with a tasty cream cheese concoction. She tried to teach me the recipe, but it included steps like straining the cranberries through a cloth. My niece, on the other hand, gave me a recipe for cranberry relish that didn't involve anything more complicated than boiling water, so that's the one I'll use to put cranberries on our table.

They'll make a colorful backdrop for displaying my applesauce.

I'm not going to put the applesauce in a serving dish. I'm putting the jar right on the table. I want everyone to read the label. It says, "I canned it myself at the Prince Edward Cannery." Me. The person with kitchen skills that revolve around sticking things in the microwave. I made real applesauce.

My adventure in this exotic undertaking began on a crisp Saturday morning in October. I arrived at the Prince Edward Cannery to take part in a "Seconds Saturday" event. Alecia Daves-Johnson from the Prince Edward County Administrator's office, ably assisted by Jennifer Samuels, introduced a group of women and one man to the facility and led us through the process of making applesauce.

We started with five bushels of Golden Delicious apples, actual Virginia-grown apples just off their trees. The first step involved slicing the apples and removing the cores. This was done by placing the apples, one by one, in the middle of a contraption that resembled a miniature guillotine. A single plunge sliced the apple flesh from its core, and tidy apple wedges fell out around it.

The next step involved boiling the apple slices in a kettle. The kettles at the Cannery don't look anything like what I've got in my kitchen. They resemble a row of shiny witches' cauldrons sitting on the floor. We didn't stir the contents with magic wands, however. We used paddles.

The real magic was what happened next. We put the boiled apples into one end of a machine that had two output spouts. One spout produced mashed apple pulp that looked remarkably like applesauce. The other spout spat out the peels.

Then we boiled the apple mash, added sugar, and sterilized jars while we waited for a thermometer to report that the mixture was done. When the moment arrived, my task was to help scoop the hot applesauce from the kettle and funnel it into jars. Other people removed air bubbles, ensured that an appropriate amount of space was left at the neck of the jar, cleaned the edges, and applied the lids. The filled jars were submerged in boiling water while we cleaned up and waited.

At the end of the morning's work, I had some sore muscles from all that slicing, stirring, and lifting. And my fingers were wrinkled and aching from washing and sanitizing equipment. But, I had six jars of applesauce and a heart filled with the kind of satisfaction that comes only from personal achievement. Yes indeed, I canned it myself at the Prince Edward Cannery. And I'm serving my applesauce for Thanksgiving. The turkey will be optional.

The Prince Edward Cannery is located at 7916 Abilene Road near Hampden-Sydney College. It opened in 1975 to serve people in the community who wanted to can farm and garden produce for home use. Equipment is on hand for processing a diverse range of fruits, vegetables, jams and jellies, meats, and fish. In 2010 the facility began an upgrading and certification process to permit the addition of commercial operations. As a result, local food entrepreneurs are now able to cook up products for resale. Cannery hours vary by season. Some days are designated for home canners and some for commercial users. Call ahead at 434-223-8664 for more information or to ask about upcoming classes.

… COLDER DAYS AND WARMER HEARTS 155

THE SEASONAL CLOCK STRIKES AUTUMN

September 2013

I woke up the morning of August 15, 2013 and headed out to the back porch with my customary cup of coffee. A chill in the air drove me back inside to fetch a sweater. Apparently the seasons were starting to change. A few days later, this was confirmed when I noted a handful of yellow leaves atop a tulip poplar at the edge of my yard.

The signs of summer's impending departure had been around for weeks, but I had overlooked them. There were "Back to School" advertisements in the newspaper, but having no school-aged children, I just ignored them. A promotion for ordering Christmas cards arrived in my mailbox. I scoffed and tossed it in the trash. I should have taken these signs as fair notice that summer was waning.

Usually, I'm more in touch with the passing seasons. During a typical summer, I spend as many nights as possible out under the stars. Their movement indicates where the earth is in its yearly cycle and keeps me abreast of major shifts to come. This year, however, we've experienced such a long string of cloudy and rainy nights that the stars moved on unobserved.

One of the constellations associated with seasonal change is Virgo, a long stick-figure like arrangement of stars that many ancient cultures viewed as a young woman. Virgo plays a role in a Greco Roman story about Demeter (alternatively called Ceres), the goddess of agriculture, and her daughter, Persephone (or Proserpina). As the story goes, Persephone was so beautiful, the god of the underworld stole the girl and carted her off to be his bride. Overcome by grief at the loss of her daughter, Demeter neglected her duties, and the people of earth were plunged into perpetual winter. Eventually, the other gods and goddesses negotiated a solution to the crisis. The divinities agreed that Persephone would spend half the year in the underworld with her husband and half the year with her mother. Correspondingly, Virgo spends the spring and summer months in the night sky. As fall approaches, the constellation slips toward the horizon, ultimately disappearing from the evening until it rises again the following spring.

My favorite constellation for marking earth's seasons is Ursa Major, more commonly known as the Big Bear. Because of the earth's orientation in space, this constellation seems to revolve in a counterclockwise motion around the North Star. From our latitude, it never disappears below the horizon. As it rotates in this circular fashion, it functions as a seasonal clock. According to a Native American story, the Big Bear emerges from its den in the spring when the constellation swings up from the horizon. As the year moves forward, it mounts ever higher in the sky. Three stars follow it. In Greco Roman stories, which also see a bear in this area of the sky, these three stars are identified as the bear's tail. They are also sometimes called the "handle" of the Big Dipper (a group of stars that comprises part of the larger bear). In the Native American version of the story, these three stars are hunters chasing the bear. Sharp-eyed observers may note a dim companion sitting next to the middle star. This is the pot in which the hunters plan to cook the bear. As the year and the hunt both progress, the bear finally tires. In late summer, it descends toward the horizon. When the hunters' arrows pierce the bear in autumn, its blood paints the trees causing leaves to turn crimson. The bear's skeleton rests along the horizon until spring, when a bear rises from its den to begin the hunt once more.

These celestial markers are a more certain indicator of the year's progress than the vagaries of temperature and cloud cover or even cyclical shopping experiences. And even though we're sure to have many more temperate, sunny days in the months ahead, those days will assuredly be shorter and the nights longer than those of the departing summer. I've been forewarned, and I've got my coat and scarf on standby.

KIDS THESE DAYS
November 2013

Recently I participated in an uncomfortable discussion. One person in the group talked about "kids these days" in a disparaging way. I had to step in and disagree because the young folks I've met are actually wonderful people. They are perhaps the best-educated generation our nation has ever seen, and their connections to the world give them an unsurpassed awareness of globally important issues. In addition, those I've met have been consistently kind and generous.

The Farmville community plays host to thousands of young people who come to study at Longwood University and Hampden-Sydney College. Every fall, they return bringing revitalizing energy and enthusiasm. Notably, many lend their hands to help lighten the burden felt by volunteers in local community service organizations.

One young woman I met while volunteering during a Saturday distribution at the local food pantry was a criminal justice major at Longwood. She talked about her aspirations to make a difference in the ways our nation seeks to rehabilitate offenders. Another student I met was a photographer who hoped that her art would someday inspire people to take better care of each other and the world around them. I've even had the privilege of talking with a young man who had his eyes set on a run for the U.S. presidency. As I listened to his thoughts on domestic and international issues, I was ready to cast my vote his way.

I also remember an encounter with a young man on the Hampden-Sydney campus. I arrived to attend a class offered by Central Virginia Arts, and I was lost. I had managed to find a parking place near the appropriate building, but the edifice itself presented a rather daunting front. I wasn't able to identify even which door I was supposed to go through. I approached a student. He graciously pointed and started telling me which interior stairways and hallways I'd have to navigate. Then he stopped himself. "I think I'd better show you." And he did. Whatever errand he'd been doing for himself, he set it aside and took a few minutes to help me get to my class on time. I don't know if HSC awards grades for impressing campus visitors, but I would have given this guy an A.

Last fall, as a member of the Friends of High Bridge Trail State Park, I had an opportunity to work with some Longwood students enrolled in Project Success, which is a class that helps students learn about leadership and citizenship. During that semester, the students helped organize and conduct a Veterans Day program in the park. I saw their passion for getting things done and their eagerness to serve the community. Their efforts helped make the program a resounding success.

Students from Longwood and HSC also regularly participate in an annual, nation-wide program called The Big Event, a special day set aside for community service. If I add up the numbers posted on the websites of both schools, I find that last year more than 800 students worked on nearly 100 different job sites throughout Farmville and the surrounding communities.

To be sure, occasionally a student or small group of students will do something insanely stupid and make the headlines. These isolated incidents are exceptions. Unfortunately, such notoriety tends to obscure a myriad of other stories about the vast majority who do marvelous things. Here's just one more example among many: Through Longwood's popular program, Alternative Spring Break, students give their vacation time to go and help people who face conditions such as inadequate housing and extreme poverty. In spring 2014, some of Longwood's students went to the Dominican Republic and others to places of need within the U.S.

The "kids these days" are abundant. They're all around town. They are our next generation of leaders. We, their elders, have given them a mess to contend with, but based on my observations, the future is in good hands.

According to tradition, this is the time of year for being thankful. I'd like to go on the record and give thanks to and for the current generation of rising adults.

TRADITIONS WORTH KEEPING
December 2009

This will be our first Christmas in Farmville. To our delight, all of our children plan to come and spend the holiday with us in our new home.

The bittersweet reality of being in a new place, however, is that some pieces of our traditional celebration will get left behind. For example, I'm not sure what to do with the Christmas stockings. Typically, as the old poem suggests, we've hung them by the chimney with care. Here, we've got no chimney. And, because our time together will be so short, we probably won't spend it making our annual gingerbread house. Church activities will be different as we head for Christmas Eve services without extended family. Perhaps most difficult of all, no one will make the drive across town to fetch Grandma, because she's now several states away.

To help focus on what matters the most, we considered the elements of our past celebrations to see which ones held the greatest significance for each of us.

For me, it was Christmas lights. They remind me that Jesus is the light of the world. Even through the longest nights, His light shines. My husband mentioned our nativity set. Among the stable's usual sheep and cattle, we add a few turtles and a platypus. They proclaim that the miracle of Christmas is available to all. We complete the scene with a Santa, hat off, kneeling beside the manger—a reminder that the commercial aspects of the season are pointless unless they bow to the child whose birth we celebrate.

Our oldest son wanted food. Christmas dinner. A kitchen filled with hustle and bustle. He wants familiar carols playing in the background as aromas mingle together and helping hands join in various tasks. His helping hands, it must be noted, tend toward mischief. One year after being asked to put the leaves in the dining room table, he reported back that the job was finished. When I arrived with a festive tablecloth, I laughed to see the table gaping open, a strand of artificial ivy draped across its center. Yes, I acknowledged. I did say "leaves." Now our tradition is to ask someone else to put the leaves in the table, but the story has become part of our family lore. This sharing of memories and telling family stories is really what he wants when he says he wants Christmas dinner.

My daughter insisted on a Christmas tree overflowing with all the decorations we've accumulated in nearly three decades. Many are homemade trinkets crafted from fabric or Styrofoam and adorned with sequins, pins, and ribbon. Some are just scraps of paper pasted together by tiny fingers. There are also commemorative keepsakes and a smattering of ornaments that joined our collection as great-grandparents passed them on. Topping it all, anticipating the birth of the infant in Bethlehem, we have a smiling star of felt and buttons. My daughter is right. The tree certainly stays.

Our youngest was the most direct: Presents. I know him well enough to understand that he didn't mean this in a selfish, "What am I going to get?" way, but rather that he looks forward to the excitement, suspense, and surprise that wrapped packages bring. He also has a generous spirit and savors the joy of giving. This year, with the economy as it is and with fewer people gathered around, there will be fewer packages under our tree, but I agree with him that the gifts are important. After all, the entire purpose of Christmas is to remember that "God so loved the world that He gave His only begotten Son, that whosoever believeth in him should not perish but have everlasting life" (John 3:16). Jesus, the greatest gift of all, reaches out and gives to others with our hands.

Whatever pieces make up the traditions you embrace at this special time of year, from our family to yours, we wish you a very blessed holiday season.

REFLECTIONS
December 2010

On a recent Sunday morning, I attended one of the many fine local churches. This particular church follows a traditional form of worship, featuring clergy and choir in vestments along with an assortment of robed young people of diverse ages who assist in various functions.

At one point during the service, a small procession made its way into the midst of the congregation for a reading from the Bible. The first person in the procession carried a cross. She was flanked by two other participants bearing ornate brass candleholders. The person who would read the text brought up the rear.

The procession stopped at a point where one of the young people carrying a candle stood just at the end of the pew where I was sitting. He was about five or six years old. The top of his head came up nearly as high as the back of the pew.

The reading commenced, but I was distracted by this young one who was likewise distracted. He caught a glimpse of himself in the intricate swells and curves of the polished gleam of the candlestick. From my vantage point, I couldn't see his view of his reflection. But I could see him. With characteristic movements, he acted just like all children do upon encountering fun-house mirrors. He stretched, holding his head as high as he could. Then he pulled it down between hunched shoulders. He nodded and bobbed from side to side.

I could imagine the image he saw. A long skinny neck. An elongated oval for a head. Then a pinhead. I wondered if any particular angle rendered his view of himself upside down or if there were a point where his head appeared to separate from his body.

After a few minutes of head angle adjustments, he began to experiment with facial expressions. He opened his eyes wide and tested eyebrow movements and nostril flares. It wasn't long before he added an impressive range of lip curls, grimaces, and scowls.

He was testing the limits of tongue extensions when the reading abruptly stopped. After just the briefest hesitation, he resumed a dignified demeanor and marched his candlestick back to the front of the sanctuary.

I can't tell you what Bible passage was read, and the young man whose antics I had watched probably can't tell you either. Nevertheless, I think we both learned important lessons.

He discovered some elemental truths about the inner workings of light and how it reflects off oddly shaped surfaces. I hope he continues to observe the world around him, finding innovative ways of interacting with it. I hope his parents and teachers guide him in his quest to understand the shape and limits of physical reality. Perhaps someday he'll be a physicist who uncovers new dimensions of this wonder-filled creation in which we live.

I gained insight into how God's light reflects off imperfect surfaces. The Bible claims that Jesus is the light of the world, and I wondered what people see when his light reflects off me. Do my actions make it sometimes seem to others that the God I worship must be a pinhead? Or, does he somehow cast his light in a way that compensates for my foibles?

I recalled the Bible verse in which Jesus admonishes his followers to "Let your light so shine before men, that they may see your good works and glorify your father who is in heaven" (Matthew 5:16). I thought about the fact that if I shine any light at all it is merely a reflection of his.

At this time of year, it seems fitting to remember that many of our neighbors, fellow countrymen, and indeed many people in diverse places and situations around the globe are facing the darkest hours of their lives. If you doubt this, just watch a newscast. But even if you feel as imperfect and as small as I feel, and no matter what faith or philosophy you embrace, surely there must still be moments when even our imperfections can help bring something into focus for someone else.

This holiday season, let your light shine.

SUCH A SMALL THING
December 2011

The power of tiny things has been very much on my mind. With good cause. One Saturday morning last month, I rolled over and the room started spinning. The ceiling light whirled round and round. Gravity seemed unreliable. I shut my eyes and held onto the side of the mattress to keep from falling off the planet. The slightest movement caused the world around me to resume its spiraling frenzy. I recalled the old David Bowie song featuring an astronaut who drifted off into space, and I feared a similar fate.

With my husband's help, I managed to get dressed. He drove me to the emergency department at Centra Southside Hospital. The attending doctor made an immediate diagnosis. He said I had a classic, textbook case of something called benign positional vertigo. He explained that it was caused by the displacement of small rocks in the inner ear. In medical terms, these rocks are called otoliths. They are composed of limestone and protein. When the otoliths are positioned where they belong, they enable a person to maintain balance. Misplaced, they send incorrect signals to the brain about the body's orientation in space. The brain tries to reconcile false information from the affected ear with accurate information from the unaffected ear. This creates a sensation of uncontrolled spinning.

Rocks in my head! My children have probably suspected this all along, but it came as a surprise to me.

I wondered about the size of these rocks. According to Timothy C. Hain, MD, a doctor specializing in dizziness (http://www.dizziness-and-balance.com), their size in humans ranges from 3 to 30 microns with an average size of 10 microns. Apparently fish have them too, and they're a lot bigger in fish—big enough to measure on a ruler in fractions of an inch.

For the human size, however, I couldn't envision how big a micron was. I knew the definition, that a micron was one-millionth of a meter, but that was too abstract a concept. I had a ruler that included centimeters (hundredths of meters) and millimeters (thousandths of meters), but that still didn't help me envision the size of something that might be as tiny as 3 millionths of a meter.

Turning to the internet for help, I found the site of a company called Industrial Specialities Manufacturing. They explained that a micron was about 1/25,000 of an inch. That meant a line of 2,500 otoliths with an average size of 10 microns would measure one inch. I started to get a vague feeling for how small these things were.

I looked farther and found other micron comparisons from Clearstream Filters, Inc. According to them, the limit of visibility is about 40 microns. In other words, even a large human otolith at 30 microns is too small to be seen with the unaided eye. For comparison, a human hair is about 70 microns in diameter. An average otolith of 10 microns compares with a single grain of talcum powder. At the small end, an otolith of 3 microns is between one-quarter and one-third the size of a red blood cell.

So as rocks go, otoliths are indeed teeny. But for being such small things, they certainly have a dramatic effect on a person's perception of the entire world. That fact led me to think about how other seemingly small things can have huge effects. How a teacher's kind word can inspire a career or how a gentle touch of the hand can turn despair into hope. A Biblical parable identifies a mustard seed as the smallest of garden seeds, and it says that faith of even this tiny size can change the world.

When I think about the size of the entire earth, I wonder if a person by comparison might be about the size of an otolith. And then I remember that one small child born more than 2,000 years ago certainly put his spin on all of history. As I prepare to celebrate the remembrance of his birth, I wish you and your family a Merry Christmas and a happy holiday season.

AT THE CALENDAR'S END
December 2012

The Mayan Long Count Calendar rolled over to usher in a new era on December 21, 2012. At first, some feared the future would be cancelled—"The End." But most prognosticators expected that the practice of counting days would simply continue.

Around the world and throughout history, cultures have established different cycles and counted beginnings and renewals in many different ways. For example, in the United States, the Gregorian calendar with its twelve unequal months identifies the days in the civil year. It is a solar-based system that defines a year as the time it takes the earth to travel around the sun and return to a starting point. The Gregorian year begins on January 1 and concludes on December 31. The Islamic calendar operates on a different principle. It counts months by the moon. Because the lunar cycle doesn't match the solar cycle, months in the Islamic system migrate through the seasons as years move forward. It takes 33 years for the seasonal cycle to return to the point where it started.

The mystery and fascination associated with the Mayan calendar center on its longevity. Researchers estimate that its beginning can be found on a date that would have fallen in 3114 BC using the Gregorian calendar's system of calculation. This means that the Mayan Long Count Calendar spanned a time frame of 5,126 solar years. Contrasted with how quickly things seem to become obsolete in modern times, a calendar that needs renewing only once every five thousand or so years feels remarkably stable.

When I was a child, my father would hang a 12-month calendar in the kitchen so that we could conveniently fix our place in time and see what was coming up—like my birthday: Would it fall on a good day for a party? The calendar usually featured an advertisement from the local hardware or five and dime, and it watched over all our days for the entire year. When the Christmas decorations went up, the new calendar would be placed behind the old so you could peek ahead if necessary. When the Christmas decorations came down, the old year went out with the trash and the new year waited to be explored.

Somewhere along the way, year-long calendars became multi-paged creations. At first, the pages were affixed to a permanent image for the year and each month was simply torn off and thrown away after its days were used up. Then came calendars where each month had its own picture. By the time one image started feeling comfortably familiar, it was time to embrace another.

After that, a weekly appointment calendar found its way to my desk top, and I started flipping pages at a breakneck speed. Now my appointments are all on my phone where a retro-looking flip clock ushers me into the future one moment at a time. Some days it seems I can't even breathe before I'm supposed to be doing the next thing.

One organization, called The Long Now Foundation (http://long now.org), noticed the ever-increasing pace of modern life and fretted about the consequences of focusing exclusively on the short-term. They began working on a project to produce a mechanical clock that would track time for 10,000 years. When complete, their clock will stand 200 feet high and provide astronomical data along with the time and date for the next ten millennia.

At 10,000 years, The Long Now Foundation's clock will nearly double the duration of the Mayan calendar—which outlived the civilization that created it. I wonder if anyone will be around to marvel at its last chimes. It certainly won't be me, but the thought that it might be someone does stir me to imagine what the world could be in the distant future and to consider the potential legacy of the era in which I live.

So as the last days of the year and the hectic holidays approach, I find myself seeking a longer-term perspective, a perspective that stands in awe on the brink of eternity. And from this place, I wish you holiness for your holidays and inspiration for all your new beginnings.

SENDING SEASONAL GREETINGS
December 2013

One of my favorite Christmas-related tasks is sending greeting cards to friends and family members. The job begins with selecting the cards. I visit stores and look at pictures. I read solicitations from organizations offering cards as part of their fund-raising plans. I enjoy seeing all the beautiful winter scenes, silly reindeer cartoons, cute animals, thoughtful religions messages, and widespread hopes for a better world.

Sometimes one with a particularly striking image or a perfectly expressed sentiment will capture my attention, but usually it's so hard to choose one I end up with a box of this and a box of that. This year I opted for boxes of assorted cards, so I'll have to spend some extra time addressing envelopes to make sure I select the best for each recipient.

Addressing the envelopes can be a bittersweet task. There are joys, such as remembering who got married, who had a new baby, and who moved into a new home. But there is also sadness. Because removing the names of people who passed away feels like such an official good-bye, I often procrastinate. It can take me years to actually delete a name from my address book. Encountering these loitering names gives me a chance to recall happy times, but it also touches lingering spots of grief. And, there are other places on the list with concerns of their own. Divorces change "Mr. and Mrs." to Mr. and Ms. at separate addresses. Some names belong to people whose health is failing, whose jobs have evaporated, or whose families include members struggling with addictions. The task of addressing the envelopes gives me an opportunity to think about the situations and to offer up short prayers.

The most delightful part of the job involves composing our traditional Christmas letter. Since the advent of digital photography, the text portion has shrunk to just a sentence or two. The difficult part is choosing the pictures. It's an activity that compels me to recall an entire year's worth of good times. Technically, I could look at my pictures without the impetus of the Christmas letter, but I know I wouldn't. There would be too many other things to do with too many other deadlines. The pictures would remain in their file folders, unviewed, unremembered. The memories would languish, and then they'd be forgotten.

For a while, I toyed with the idea of stopping the tradition of including a Christmas letter with our cards because some people seemed to think the practice was somewhat outmoded and vain. Once someone told me she didn't like Christmas letters. "They don't tell what's real. They're so cheesy. It's an obnoxious form of bragging," she complained.

Some people even claim there's a virtue in not sending Christmas cards. They grumble about the trees that are cut down. They complain about the fossil fuels burned by postal delivery vehicles. They prattle about the cost of stamps, money that could have been donated to help feed the hungry. They claim it's more efficient to tweet a seasonal greeting and post photos on a Facebook page.

I can't argue with all that logic, but I think sharing life's joys and good times is a way to help spread happiness. And although I recognize the value of efficiency and the need to be environmentally aware, I still prefer the quainter technology of paper and ink.

For many years, my husband and I sent cards to a relative who had chosen to isolate himself after a quarrel with other family members. We never received a card back. He never attended any family gatherings. When this relative died, we continued to send cards to his widow. Later, we encountered her at a funeral. She thanked us for all the years of cards. "That was the only family contact I had," she explained. "It meant a lot." Perhaps that's why the process of sending the cards means a lot to me.

So, cheesy or not, I plan to continue composing Christmas letters and sending out cards. May your holidays be blessed with the traditions and people you hold most dear.

… CHRISTMAS TIME 169

THE STAR OF BETHLEHEM
December 2015

Several months ago during an astronomy event at High Bridge Trail State Park, I pointed out some of the sights overhead. I retold a couple ancient stories associated with some of the constellations, and I mentioned the names of some of the sky's brightest stars. Afterward, a park visitor approached and asked if I would please also indicate which one was the Star of Bethlehem, the star that directed the Magi to the stable where Jesus was born.

According to the second chapter of Matthew's gospel, wise men saw a certain star, and by its rising, they realized a king of the Jewish people had been born. Guided by the star, they ultimately came to a place where they found the child and his mother. After bestowing gifts, they departed.

Exactly what the Magi saw and followed remains a mystery, yet theories abound.

One suggestion is that the Star of Bethlehem was actually a comet. There are many different kinds of comets. Periodic comets, also known as short-term comets, are perhaps the best known because their orbits bring them into view on a regular schedule. Halley's Comet, for example, shows up every 76 years. Long-period comets, on the other hand, can take millions of years to complete a single orbit. Hyperbolic comets may pass through the inner solar system only once. After that single visit, the sun's gravitational force hurls the comet into the vastness of interstellar space. Sun-grazing comets have orbits that take them perilously close to the sun. Sometimes they survive the solar encounter, and sometimes they do not.

Comets also present a wide variety of appearances. History records several notable comets that were sufficiently bright to be seen by day. Although none have been that bright in recent decades, there have been a few that put on respectable night-time displays. They could be seen by almost anyone who cared to look up. Other comets have been dimmer, and spotting them required a trained eye or optical aids.

So far, attempts to match the timing of a known, short-term comet with the appearance of the Star have been unsuccessful, but the number of other comet candidates is virtually endless. Maybe the Magi saw a long-period comet, a hyperbolic comet, a comet that no longer exists, or a comet that was not apparent to untrained eyes. Perhaps. But there are other possible explanations.

Some people speculate that the Star of Bethlehem might have been a supernova. When stars of certain sizes reach the ends of their lifespans, they explode. During the explosion, the light emitted increases by fantastic amounts. The appearances of supernovae are unpredictable. The last supernova recorded in our galaxy occurred during the early seventeenth century. At its peak, it reached a brightness that surpassed that of all the other stars in the sky and rivaled Jupiter (the second brightest of the planets).

Other theories relate to planetary conjunctions, times when the planets seem close together from an Earth-bound perspective. And some people speculate that the Star of Bethlehem referred to the position of just one of the planets as it moved through a special area of the sky. Planets that are farther away from the sun than the earth, orbit the sun more slowly than the earth. Because of this, when the earth's orbit passes them, their motion seems to periodically pause and even go backwards for a time. This seems to fit the part of the Gospel account telling about the Star coming to rest.

Yet another theory proposes that the Star of Bethlehem wasn't a natural occurring celestial light at all, but that it was placed temporarily in the sky and moved supernaturally according to God's plan. Still others say the Star was a metaphor for the guidance that comes to all who seek.

In the end, my laser pointer proved inadequate for the task of identifying a specific light as the Star of Bethlehem. I couldn't tell my questioner, "There it is." But, for me, this isn't a problem. Although I can't say exactly what light led the wise men, I understand that God is the source of all light and all the stars belong to God.

STILL HAPPY, GRATEFUL TOO
November 2015

This column appears monthly under the title "Happy to Be Here." Such a public declaration leads people to question me. "You can't be happy about everything," they insist. "What don't you like?" Inquiring minds want to know.

So, in the spirit of full disclosure, I'm forced to admit that there are a few things I don't like.

For starters, there's the habit some drivers have of crossing a road's center line. To be sure, other places also have quirks when it comes to road manners. Where I used to live in southeast Michigan, for example, running red lights was a favored pastime. Here—at least for the most part—people stop on red and then wait for green. The wanton disregard for staying on one's own side of the road, however, is something I haven't encountered elsewhere, and I'm still unaccustomed to the practice. Discovering an oncoming vehicle hurtling toward me in my lane makes me gasp and sets my heart aflutter. One person with whom I discussed this phenomenon explained that he felt justified in "straightening out the curves" because he "pays taxes on both sides of the road." Frankly, I'd prefer it if people used just one side of the road at a time. That way, we can all live to enjoy the journey back home.

Another item on the list of things I don't like is the practice of flicking cigarette butts out of car windows or dropping them onto the ground. I suppose the region's tobacco heritage may give some folks the impression that cigarette butts are part of nature, but in fact they represent a huge litter problem. Cigarette butts are predominantly made of cellulose acetate (not cotton, as many suppose). Cellulose acetate is a form of plastic, and it lingers in the environment for a long time. Although each individual cigarette butt is small, they add up. Admittedly, this problem isn't unique to our area, but we live in a region with such natural beauty, it's really noticeable when virtually every roadway, every stream, and every path includes cigarette litter. (For more information, see the "Cigarette Butt Litter" section of the Clean Virginia Waterways website, hosted by Longwood University, at http://www.longwood.edu/cleanva/cigarettelitterhome.html.)

I also don't like the frequency with which so many people complain that there's "nothing to do" in Farmville. It makes me feel socially awkward when I have to disagree so intensely with a popular opinion. In my experience, there's plenty to do. In recent months, I've had opportunities to enjoy events featuring world class musicians, nationally renowned entertainers, performances by university and community ensembles, notable art displays, and collegiate sports. I can go for a long walk any time I want. Canoeing and kayaking are readily available (at least when it's warm enough). There are clubs for a diverse array of interests and volunteer organizations through which I can lend my hands to causes that are important to me. Farmville even has venues for such favored American pastimes as going bowling or out to dinner and the movies. I have to scratch my head and wonder: what more do people want?

True, there are sometimes nuisances related to living in a small community. My internet connection is slow. I can't always find the vegetables I want in the supermarket, and if I'm hankering to try Moroccan food, I have to venture beyond the borders of our town. And, there are real social issues that need to be addressed (hence my earlier comment about volunteer organizations). But, here's the reality: if a person searched the entire Earth looking for a utopia where everything was absolutely perfect, that person would come up empty handed.

When I moved here, I wasn't expecting utopia, but what I found came pretty close. I discovered warm, welcoming people who accepted me with open arms. And if I can't shop for furniture on Sunday afternoons, the consolation is that I get to stroll down a street where passersby wave greetings and friends stop to chat.

So yes, I'm happy to be here. I'm grateful to have found a place in such an amazing community.

Also available

from Karen A. Bellenir

Which Good Book?
An Impartial Guide to Choosing a Bible Translation
by Karen A. Bellenir

This interactive tool will help you select the Bible translation that best suits your needs. Available from PierPress.com/bookstore

"A profoundly helpful and very well-executed resource... Very informative on the whole nature of biblical translation... You did all this without leaving behind the average lay person in a cloud of technical language." David Jahn, Pastor, Advent Lutheran Church, Melbourne, Florida

from Pier Press

Observations:
A Monthly Newsletter from Pier Press

Each issue offers readers a chance to look up at wonders in the sky, look around to discover what science can reveal, look within to enhance spiritual life, and look ahead to see what's on the calendar.
Subscribe at PierPress.com. It's FREE.

Pier Perspectives
Curious about the universe in which you live? Eager to learn more about its material, cultural, and spiritual components? Read the Pier Perspectives, a blog available at PierPress.com/pierperspectives.

Pier Press Bookstore
The Pier Press Bookstore features Pier Press publications, such as the *Walk with the Gospel Writers* series of journals for personal sprititul discovery, and other resources. Visit PierPress.com/bookstore.

www.ingramcontent.com/pod-product-compliance
Lightning Source LLC
Chambersburg PA
CBHW052130010526
44113CB00034B/1543